The Staffieri
Principles

THE STAFFIERI PRINCIPLES

A Philosophy in Employee Management

Nick Staffieri

To order additional copies of this book, contact:
Xlibris LLC
1-888-795-4274
www.Xlibris.com
Orders@Xlibris.com
143189

CONTENTS

Chapter List

CHAPTER 1

Introduction

So you are ready to step into management. Or perhaps you already are in management. Either way, there is plenty of responsibility that comes with the title "Manager". Along with that responsibility comes a bit of stress in dealing with it all. And let's not forget that the more responsibility that you assume, or are given, the higher risk of stress comes with it.

So what is the best way to "manage" all that responsibility? Well, if it's just stress relief you are looking for, there are breathing exercises for that. (Or a heavy dose of chocolate milkshakes. Hey, that works for me.) But the whole purpose of this book is not to develop stress relief skills. After all, the best way to manage stress is to eliminate it.

Many experts will agree that when having the responsibility to manage, the most stressful part of management comes when dealing with employee problems. So when there are no employee problems, and all you have is great employees all around you, everything else comes easy. After all, great employees will take initiative to manage production, keep customers happy, resolve their own problems, etc. Wow. That sort of leaves you with nothing to worry about. Except . . .

. . . how do you get and keep great employees? I am glad you asked. Great employees are great for a reason. It's because they are managed properly. So what we just learned is that the better you manage your employees, the better they will perform for you. And that is precisely the theme of this book. Now let's take a look at how we do that.

Management: A Definition

Before we get into details about the best ways to manage employees, we must first understand what management is. To be successful at management, we must first define it. Understanding what management is will enable you to practice its functions and build a career as a Management Representative of your company.

MSN Encarta defines MANAGEMENT as:

1) Administration of business: the organizing and controlling of the affairs of a business or a particular sector of a business

2) Managers as a group: managers and employers considered collectively, especially the directors and executives of a business or organization

3) Handling of something successfully: the act of handling or controlling something successfully

4) Skill in handling or using something: the skill of handling or use of something such as resources

Let's take a look at each of the four definitions of management and expand on its meaning.

1) Administration of business is the organizing and controlling of the affairs of a business or particular sector of a business. As a manager, you are responsible for the organization and control of your area of responsibility. This could be a department of the company or a responsibility of the company such as cash flow or customer service. Whatever the department or sector of business that falls under your responsibility, your title as manager gives you direct decision making power that can, and most often will, affect the outcome of the business.

2) Managers as a group is the collective team of managers and executives of a business. In simple terms, this means that your title as Manager means that you are a part of management. This is a very

important concept to understand. As a part of management, every decision you make must conform to company policy and philosophy. You are the voice of the corporation. If such is the case, and I assure you it is, then you need to be knowledgeable of corporate policies, goals and business strategies.

3) Management is also defined as the handling of something successfully. As we look at this definition closely, we discover that the key word is successfully. Without handling it successfully, we are not managing it. Most would agree that we are mismanaging the situation.

4) The skill in handling or using something commonly refers to the use of materials or resources. Without the knowledge and skill in utilizing these, our ability to manage becomes limited. Imagine what disasters can occur if you do not properly align vendors to meet your service standards or adhere to pricing structures. By dealing with vendors and resources properly, we can keep control of service levels and operating costs thereby effectively managing your areas of responsibility.

Management Definition

The administration of business
Managers as a group
Handling of something successfully
The skill in handling or using resources

What Do We Manage

Now that we understand what MANAGEMENT is, we next need to define what it is we manage. In any business or industry, there are four critical areas of responsibility that must be managed. For any business to survive and succeed, all four areas must receive an equal amount of focus. The four critical areas of responsibility that must be managed are:

Production

Customer Service

Employees

Cost

In many organizations, the management of these critical areas of responsibility may fall under several different executives or levels of senior and middle managers. It is also a common trend that each critical area of responsibility listed above falls to a higher level of management than the next. For example, Production is typically managed by lower level managers while Customer Service may be managed by middle management. Employee Management would then be managed by senior management and Cost by executive management. However, in smaller organizations where these levels do not exist, the management of several or all of these critical areas of responsibility may fall all under one or two individuals. Whatever the size and scope of the organization, all four of these critical areas of responsibility must be managed.

Imagine being successful in managing production, customer service and employees and yet doing it all while being thousands of dollars over budget each month. The organization will not be very profitable and thereby not be successful. Likewise, being under budget each month while losing customers with poor customer service or failed production standards will likely end in disaster for the company. Without all four critical areas of responsibility being managed, the company or organization will ultimately fail. It is the function of the Management Team to sustain the organization through the proper management of all four critical areas of responsibility.

Management Development

Experience is everything when it comes to managing people. It's like any other activity. The more experience you have, the better you become at it. Experience helps develop your skill. It is the same when it comes to management development. Managing people is a critical and quite comprehensive task. Because there are so many different personalities to deal with, and so many emotions that we as individuals can express during our work day, it takes a lot of years to develop the experience in managing it all. This is why the management development process takes such a long time to master.

To begin a management development process, we must first understand certain key factors. There are three factors in understanding the management role.

 Three Key Management Factors

1. You cannot be told how to manage
2. You will not become a great manager overnight
3. Management styles must be developed over time

Key Factor #1: You cannot be told how to manage

As a manager, we are called upon to make many decisions. Some of these decisions may require great thought and analysis while others may be made in a second's notice during a critical situation. Either way, it is the manager, or a member of leadership, that makes these decisions. Once that authority is taken away and handled by someone other than the manager, the manager ceases to be managing. Remember our definition from chapter one that describes management as the ability to handle something successfully. If we are being told or directed in how to handle situations, the situation is being managed not by us, but by the person directing us. This is not to say that managers should not receive sound advice from mentors or their immediate manager. This is all a part of the development process. However, it is the manager in charge of the situation that must ultimately make the decision and be accountable for it.

When I hired a manager to manage one of the office departments, I was asked on his first day "How do you want me to manage this office?" I was confused by the question, so I answered, "The best way you can." The thought behind the answer is to address this very concept that you cannot be told how to manage. If someone in authority placed you in the position of manager, they are stating that they have trust and confidence in your ability to manage. Sure, there may be a great learning curve (see key factor number 2). But I've always preached that doing is learning. Being told what to do (and let's face it: who ever likes to be told what to do?) completely takes the authority away from you. And if you are managing employees, that is the worst thing that can happen.

Having no authority to make decisions or put ideas into practice leaves you with no real management responsibilities. Or, if you have the authority to do so but continue to rely on your boss, or someone in a higher ranking position, to handle these critical situations, you are not showing to your organization or to your employees that you have the confidence in yourself or the ability to do so. If that is the case, how can you expect your employees to have confidence in your leadership? The bottom line is: Don't be afraid to be decisive. The worst that can happen is that you make a wrong decision. Learn from it, take responsibility for it, and move forward. If it is a tough decision, it's ok to get others involved. But ultimately, the decision must be yours. After all, you are the manager.

Key Factor #2: You will not become a great manager overnight

Taking that first promotion to manager is an exciting thing. It is also a frightening thing. To think that you will be great as a manager during your first day is unrealistic. You will be faced with challenges that you haven't dealt with before, and you will make mistakes. This is all a part of the learning process. Learning from mistakes is the best way to develop your management skills. By observing how people react to your decisions and communication tactics, you can begin to process what is effective and what is totally inappropriate. Seminars and workshops, even reading this book, is a great help. But nothing can come close to experience. Remember: Learning is doing.

Many managers think that because they are very effective in one area of their non-management position responsibilities, they will make a great manager. The truth is, it is very rare that a manager has the same level of responsibility or job description as a production level employee. So just because someone is the best as a production level employee doesn't automatically translate into that individual stepping immediately into a successful role as a manager.

There are a few situations where being placed in a management role can be even more challenging.

Take the following scenario. You are an employee who works with several other co-workers in the department. You get along with everyone and have a great relationship with a few. As co-workers, you all have the same level of responsibility. Suddenly, because you do such a great job, you are promoted to Supervisor of the department. Now, your responsibility transitions to managing this group of individuals rather than simply working with them. This is a difficult transition to make because your level of relationship must change. Others may have thought they were more qualified to take the position. Still others may feel you aren't their "friend" anymore because of the management decision you now need to make. Of course, there are others who may be happy to work for you as you take your new role, but even they will begin to see the changes in you as you become more aware of your management responsibilities. Those individuals that were so great to work with suddenly feel alienated and difficult to manage.

Your first reaction to any lack of employee support may be to go on the offensive and take the "do as I say" mentality. This is the wrong approach and will only result in a further gap between you and your new employees. Or, you may appeal to their good-natured manners and ask that they give you a break and help you with your new position. This is also the wrong approach and will only result in a lack of respect for your position. Sure, they will give you a break, but they will expect you to do the same for them when they start showing up late every day. Where does that lead?

The next scenario to consider is when you are placed in a new environment to manage tenured employees. Those employees may not be so agreeable to change. Your strategy to immediately make an impact on how things get done may result in a lack of cooperation from the tenured employees who feel they know the job and the environment better than you. (And they are right!)

When confronted by these situations, the key is to first gain the respect from your new team members. Show that you are willing to work with them and learn from them regarding how they do their job and why things are done "their" way. The Management Progression Pattern is designed to work any new manager through these struggles. The Management Progression Pattern is discussed later in this chapter.

Key Factor #3: Successful management styles must be developed over time.

As we begin to discuss management styles, you will find that a particular management style reflects who you are and what you can accomplish as a manager. As you begin your management career, you may not have developed a defined style. Developing the right style for your management image will take time and experience. Likewise, managing styles that are most effective in each situation will require development. Either way, you will find that developing the most effective management style for you will be a process.

Management styles define who we are as managers. But more importantly, it is a way of creating the right environment to maximize employee performance and potential. Managing people requires development in knowing how each individual responds to your management style. For this reason, the management style must be developed around employee behaviors and responses to specific leadership and management personalities.

Management Styles

There are many different management styles, each with its degree of successfulness in certain situations. The style you develop should fit your personality as well as maximize your ability to manage employees.

Listed below are four basic management styles that have been observed over many years of study.

Participate—The participating manager becomes involved in the daily production and activity of the unit as well as with the employees. This style is most conducive to a smaller environment or lower level manager where hands-on productivity is expected or necessary. Higher level managers who practice the participation management style may not be as hands-on with production, but continue to be involved in overseeing the production and being a part of the team on the production floor. The downside to a participating managing style is that the manager tends to become too close to the employees and therefore finds it challenging when disciplinary action is necessary.

Delegate—The delegating manager acts as a dispatcher of the work processes and controls the work flow of the unit. The delegating manager usually does not take an active role in the production. Rather, he assigns work to his employees and tracks their performance to keep an accurate assessment of individual and team productivity. The downside of the delegating manager is that he tends to separate himself from the actual production and creates an unwelcome gap between himself and his employees.

Dictate—The dictating manager is similar to the delegating manager, however, he is removed further from the work flow and production of the unit. The dictating manager can also delegate in a more stern or forceful manner usually without regard to what the current situation may be. The downside to the dictating manager is that he tends to lack the team building or employee relationship building skills necessary to effectively manage his staff. This creates a greater potential for unwanted confrontations when issues arise.

Passive—The passive manager removes himself from the daily activities of the unit and tends to strictly monitor productivity levels. The passive manager may become involved in problem resolutions, but only in a reactive manner. The passive manager allows employees to handle all levels of productivity and empowers employees to make decisions to manage the production. For a passive manager to be successful, he must ensure that his staff is well trained and motivated to perform the duties and responsibilities of the unit. Passive managers tend to shy away from personnel issues and avoid confrontation, even when apparently necessary. The downside to the passive manager is that employees may begin to take advantage of the passiveness and develop poor habits that go unaddressed. The team may lack leadership and build a gap between the manager and the staff.

 Management Styles

The key for managers to recognize is that to be an effective manager, you must develop a management style that fits the environment.

There are many management styles that a manager can develop that can be classified into one of these four categories. The key for managers to recognize is that to be an effective manager, you must develop a management style that fits the environment. That management style may have some characteristics from each of the four styles listed above.

Management styles may also change throughout the management process. Management styles may need to change based on several reasons.

Reason #1: Change in Employees—Even if you manage as little as two employees, you may find that you need to handle them differently when delegating work, training or coaching, and even disciplining them on an individual basis. Remember that every employee is an individual who will react in a uniquely different way in any given situation. Managing an entry level person who just graduated high school is far different than managing an industry veteran with 5 years to retirement. Managers must recognize what style of handling matters with each individual is most effective and gets the desired result.

Reason #2: Change in Environment that may affect the Situation—Your passive, laid back approach to management has been working great for you and your employees. Just then, your department is asked to assist with the legal department, which is a high pressure, deadline driven environment that is stressful and demanding. That passive style may not work well in motivating the team to meet the high expectations just imposed. You may need to incorporate more participating or dictating style into your management skills to meet the high demands and get your team focused on the newly established service level standards and goals.

Reason #3: Change in Industry or Business—Just because a management style is effective in one industry does not mean that you will be effective implementing that style in another. Retail management at the store level (as opposed to the Retail Corporate level) almost always needs to be participative. If you are a delegating or passive manager in a corporate environment, that style may not be received well in the retail environment where the expectations are quite different. A management style effective in the military would certainly not be as effective in the corporate environment. Changing industries or business can certainly lead to a change in management styles to be effective.

The biggest challenge with regards to management styles that managers face is the notion that all employees must "put up" or "live with" the manager's way of handling matters. This notion causes stress for both the manager and the employees. It is easier for a manager to adapt a management style around his employees than it is to expect employees to adapt to the manager's management style. Getting the best performance from employees is the ultimate goal of a manager. Use what is effective for each individual.

Management Development Progression Pattern

Every great manager has developed their management skill through learning and experience. Great managers are not born. Many experts on the subject do believe that management traits can be learned and developed with the right discipline and guidance. Others may believe that to become a great manager, one must be born with innate qualities that become exposed during the management development process. Regardless of the two beliefs, one thing is certain. Anyone can become a manager by acquiring the title. This title can be given due to factors that have nothing to do with innate qualities or learning and experience. Seniority, for example, can be a reason why one individual is promoted above others. An external hire based on a resume and interview, with or without the existence of formal reference checks, can also be a reason why an individual is placed in a position to manage others. It can be, and often times is, determined by how well an individual performs in his or her current role. This individual knows the most about the operation and is most skilled in the production. Therefore, the title of manager is quickly inherited upon him. All these situations can quickly hurdle someone to the position. But labeling someone "Manager" does not, and never will, be the factor in determining whether that person will be a good manager.

To be able to manage effectively, there must be a development progression. Even the most seasoned and successful managers can come into a new situation and fail. This is because they do not realize that a development progression must be followed. Respect from past successful performances can be a great start in these situations, but without re-establishing the progression that made the individual successful in the past, it will be difficult to maintain.

With this in mind, following the Management Development Progression Pattern whenever a new manager, or a manager entering a new management situation, will help establish the relationship between manager and subordinates. There are three levels of the Management Progression Plan. It is easiest to see how these levels develop into the next by taking it from the top of the management development chain.

These are the three progression steps that lead to management success.

- Management Demands Leadership—To be a great manager, you must first be a great leader. Establishing leadership qualities will build co-worker confidence in your ability to lead. Leadership is defined as "the ability to guide, direct, or influence people". (Source: MSN Encarta) It doesn't matter in which direction you lead, whether your intention is good or evil. It matters that you have people that believe in you and will trust that you can guide them to achieve a common goal. Once you have established that belief and trust from those you lead, you can then manage them. (For the purposes of this book, we tend to assume the intention is good and not evil.)

- Leadership Demands Discipline—A good leader does not force others to follow. A good leader earns the privilege of leading through the actions, examples and words used in the carrying out of responsibilities. For this, you must have discipline. Discipline is defined as "a conscious control over behavior" or "the ability to behave in a controlled and calm way even in a difficult or stressful situation". (Source: MSN Encarta) You must have discipline to be accountable for what falls under your responsibility. You must have discipline to act ethically and professionally while carrying out your duties. You must have discipline to do what is right and say what is right and have self-motivation to achieve success. You must have discipline to stay true to a common goal even though obstacles may block the way. This discipline will be respected among your peers and with your superiors. With that, you can then begin to lead.

- Discipline Demands Character and Integrity—This is the basis for self-discipline. Great character and integrity is essential for anyone who wants to begin or maintain a career in leadership. Without good character and integrity, you do not have the ethical mentality to become disciplined. We all know right from wrong. Integrity is the ability to choose right over wrong and character is the distinctive qualities of a person that dictate predictable actions. Character is built upon the level of integrity one possesses. You must have the moral and ethical mentality to maintain your integrity. And if you do that consistently, you can build solid character which translates into reputation. That character and reputation then motivates an individual to maintain their discipline. Integrity is not just choosing right over wrong sometimes. It must be all the time. For once the integrity is lost, a little slip in judgment, it becomes so difficult to regain it. Building trust takes great effort over a great period of time. Destroying trust takes one brief second caused by a lie or unethical action.

 Management Development Progression Pattern

Management demands Leadership
Leadership demands Discipline
Discipline demands Character and Integrity

This pattern illustrates the path to good management. You must first establish good character and integrity to establish discipline. Without good character and integrity, you cannot establish your discipline and self-discipline. Once discipline is established, you can then establish your leadership qualities. People, and in this case your employees, need to see discipline in their leaders before deciding to follow. Then you must develop and illustrate your leadership qualities before becoming a good manager. Management without leadership is an ineffective method for gaining acceptance from employees. This acceptance becomes important to lead a team and build their confidence in your focus and vision. Without this progression, proper management cannot be possible.

The Greatest Development Tool

As we explained earlier in this chapter, learning from mistakes is the best way to become a better manager. Experience is everything when it comes to gaining a comfort level and becoming better at what you do. Learn from your experiences as a manager and as an employee. We can learn just as much from bad experiences as we can from good ones. There are several exercises that can help develop our sense of management and the skills we need to possess to become a great manager.

Bad Manager Traits—Almost all of us has had a bad experience with a manager in our work history. It may not have been a bad manager, but just a bad or annoying trait about him or her that bothered us. Remember how those traits made you feel as an employee and try to avoid such traits as you begin to develop your management style.

Good Manager Traits—Just the same, we should emulate good management traits from our current and former bosses. These experiences teach us a lot about what makes employees build trust and respect for those who are in higher levels of responsibility.

Role Models—We all looked up to someone with reverence at least once in our lives. What was it about that person that drove us to feel that way? Now think about yourself as the role model for those who may look to you for guidance. Set the example as those before you did.

Mentors—Seek out mentors in your area of industry or profession. Don't hesitate to ask questions regarding the secrets to their success and what they can offer you to help you achieve your goal. Always look above you to motivate yourself. Compare yourself to the best and find out what it takes to be there with them.

> "It takes great patience to view the world from another's eyes, and great wisdom to learn from it." = Nick Staffieri, CMDSM

These exercises can help you build a better understanding of what you need to develop to become a great manager. But most importantly, you should never stop learning. There is no limit to our abilities until we stop trying to exceed that which we have already accomplished.

Chapter Review:

Management: A Definition—Defining management will help us better understand management

What Do We Manage: Production, Customer Service, Employees, Cost

Management Development: You cannot be told how to manage, You will not become a great manager overnight, Management styles must be developed over time

Management Styles: Participate, Delegate, Dictate, Passive

Management Development Progression Pattern: Management Demands Leadership, Leadership Demands Discipline, Discipline Demands Character and Integrity

The Greatest Development Tool: Learn from experience

Chapter 2

Beginners Guide to Managing Employees

It is difficult to understand how many philosophies regarding promotions disregard all concepts of proper management development. Think about it. An employee does a great job with production skills and customer service skills. He exceeds all performance goals, has a stellar attendance record and gets along well with co-workers. Because he has done so well in his current position, he is rewarded with a promotion to manager. This is a difficult situation to place an individual in without any guidance or management development.

To help in this matter, it is important for the individual in such a position to understand the responsibility level that a manager must have. Knowing this information can help the employee be better prepared to handle situations that call for management action. Or yet, help the employee decide whether or not the new management position is a right fit. After all, an employee must be willing to accept the role.

With this in mind, listed below are the top 5 reasons why an employee may not want to accept the role as manager.

Top 5 Reasons Why NOT To Get Promoted To Manager

Reason #5—I can't afford to keep buying tissues every time someone comes crying to me.

If you feel that this is not in your job description, then perhaps that position of managing people just isn't for you. Managing people requires understanding of human feelings and emotions. The greatest quality of a manager is compassion. As a manager, when you show compassion, you illustrate your concern for the person rather than just for what he or she provides to the organization as an employee. In return, that employee will gain a tremendous respect and loyalty, which is something that cannot be measured on a quality management or six sigma report.

Personal stories are not the only things a manager will hear about from employees. Employees will complain about many great things about their job as well. An employee may have a problem with another employee, a customer or even a decision you made. These complaints will no doubt reach your doorway. The first order of business is to listen. Then respond. If listening to these complaints isn't something you can handle, managing employees may not be the best career move for you.

Reason #4—Employees will expect me to solve all their problems.

Employees want to know that you are the resource that can find all the answers and solutions. Of course, you empower your employees to solve problems and make sound decisions, but when all else fails, they will no doubt head straight for your doorway expecting you to be a savior. And as their manager, you must come through for them or lose valuable respect and confidence from the people you rely on most. This is a difficult responsibility to master. Employee expectations will not change based on the position you hold. They will only change based on the person holding that position. If you can't solve their problems, you will not be effective in leading them.

If the employees have empowerment to solve their own problems, more often than not will they come to you after all their ideas are exhausted. This can make it challenging because crucial time may have already ticked away while they were out trying to solve the problem on their own. This is a good sign that they have already thought things through, but now it puts you in a position to have quick and decisive answers. After all, that is why they've come to you.

Remember that in these situations, the employee is looking for an answer to a problem. Getting the solution is the number one priority. If you begin to analyze what went wrong and who is to blame, employees will feel less comfortable bringing these problems to you in the future. If this is your goal, you will lose your approachability with your employees. If you think that is a good thing, managing employees may not be the best career move for you.

Reason #3—Customers will expect me to solve all their problems.

Customers have a right to expect this from a manager. As defined in chapter 1, you are a part of the organization's management team. With that comes a certain level of responsibility that includes deciding to enforce a policy or bending the rule to resolve a customer complaint. Customers expect you to be the decisive authority figure to resolve all their differences with the company. Knowing what your limitations are in relation to your level of management becomes important. More importantly is your ability to rationalize whether the problem resolution is within your power or not. Either way, providing the solution is your responsibility to the customer. If you are not ready to handle that responsibility, customers will likely move on to someone who can help them. And in their eyes, that makes you just another employee of the company.

Customers will also likely bring complaints to you about your employees. Sometimes, customer problems are issues they experience with employees. Customers do not want to hear how it happened or why it happened. They want to know that something will be done in response to their problem.

Solving customer problems is a major part of managing the customer service aspect of your responsibilities. If this is a responsibility you do not wish to have, managing employees may not be the best career move for you.

Reason #2—Upper Management will expect me to solve all their problems.

Yes, it's true. When Upper Management discovers a problem in your area of responsibility, they will expect you to become involved in the solution. Executive Management bases success on productivity, revenue and profitability. When any one of these are affected by your management of the production, customer service or employees, Senior level members of the organization will require your quick action to regain productivity, revenue and profitability. What are you doing and how are you going to fix it? This is the basic question that will be asked.

Executive management has a great responsibility to uphold the financial stability of the company and set direction for its future. This is far too great a responsibility for this level of leadership to focus on production and employee management. When executive management finds that something is disrupting that financial stability or future outlook, they look towards middle management to figure out what is causing the disruption. Then they expect it to be fixed. Your responsibility as a manager is to manage the four areas discussed in chapter 1. (Production, Customer Service, Employees, Cost) Managing your employees is the key to managing all other areas. If things don't get fixed, your decisions regarding employee management begin to be questioned.

So in other words, if Executive Management sees a problem, they expect you to fix it. And the best way to fix it is to have employees become more engaged and involved in the success of the company. If you don't agree with this concept, managing employees may not be the best career move for you.

Reason #1—I will be accountable for everyone and everything.

This is quite possibly the most important aspect of anyone with the title of Manager. When things go wrong, accountability shifts upwards. When the entry level associate sends out the wrong packets to field officers, the Manager must take ownership of the error and handle damage control. When an employee trips over a box and begins a workers compensation claim, the Manager must be accountable for maintaining updated safety regulations for the office. When an angry employee barks foul language in front of the customer, the only question will be "How can the Manager allow this to happen and what is he going to do about it?"

Number Two on this list states that Upper Management will want you to solve all their problems. This is because they realize that Number One on this list is an accurate description of your job. You are accountable for everything that falls under your leadership. Manage it by being in control of every aspect and you will be successful. Fail to maintain control of everything under your leadership results in non-conformances that can be costly to the organization and to your position as Manager.

Top 5 Reasons Why NOT to Get Promoted to Manager

5. I can't afford to keep buying tissues every time someone comes crying to me
4. Employees will expect me to solve all their problems
3. Customers will expect me to solve all their problems
2. Upper management will expect me to solve all their problems
1. I WILL BE ACCOUNTABLE FOR EVERYONE AND EVERYTHING

Keep in mind the philosophy of great leaders: When things are going great, it is the employees that should receive all the credit. When things are going poorly, it is the Manager that should receive all the blame. This sounds quite unfair. It may also sound like a thankless position to be in. But once implemented, you will receive thanks from those most important to your career reputation: Your employees.

Managing Employees Checklist

Managing employees is a difficult thing to master. To do it properly, we must first focus on all of the key areas that encompass employee management. There are ten key areas of personnel supervision that must be managed.

Training—Every employee needs proper training to perform their duties. Management's responsibility is to provide that training on all necessary skills. Managers must give the employee the skills and tools relative to their job responsibilities. Continuous training is also important when new processes are implemented, new technology is introduced or new services are made available. Cross training for all employees is also a key concept. This is the practice of training employees on the job responsibilities of their co-workers so that teamwork and absentee coverage can flow within your unit.

Coaching and development—Managers must ensure that the employee is heading in the right direction. Feedback on the employee's progress should include constructive criticism and proper guidance to give the employee the right mental outlook. When the employee makes a mistake, correct coaching and development can help the employee learn from the mistake and become a key contributor to the operation.

> When the employee makes a mistake, correct coaching and development can help the employee learn from the mistake and become a key contributor to the operation.

Scheduling—Building a winning team sometimes means creating schedules that fit each employee's personality. We all know that some of us can't seem to function properly until 9am while others are much too full of cheer at 7 in the morning. It is important to recognize who on the team will function better during work shifts. But scheduling does not simply mean creating work shifts or coffee breaks. Scheduling work flow and who should handle what projects throughout the day is equally necessary to operate at optimum efficiency. By understanding current schedules, a manager can analyze the effectiveness of their place in the work day. Be aware of how your schedules integrate with the rest of the organization. Do not hesitate to make changes to operate more effectively within the organizational goals.

Managing schedules can sometimes seem quite easy. We know what time certain work projects should be done and we know how to assign people to perform the tasks. We can fit employees into work shifts that best utilize their skills and best keeps the operation running from open to close. But when things go wrong, such as an employee calling out sick, three major projects hitting your desk at once or a mandate from corporate that no further overtime is to be granted, scheduling can become quite challenging. Managing these schedules, from employee shifts to project management, is vital to maintain sanity in the workplace.

Delegation—Once the employees have mastered the job skills, they are then capable of having tasks delegated to them. Whether it is primary assigned tasks that the employee will perform everyday or special projects that come up every now and then, delegation of tasks is something that must be managed properly. A manager must delegate evenly and wisely. Delegating unfairly could cause dissension. Delegating tasks totally unrelated to an employee's responsibilities could be perceived as dumping. As a manager, it is a great skill to know when to delegate, what to delegate and to whom to delegate.

Motivation—Simply delegating tasks to an employee isn't enough. As managers, we must be prepared to motivate the employee to perform the tasks. There are many ways to motivate employees and many employees that are motivated in different ways. Employees need to know what the incentives are for performing the work. They also need to feel a sense of responsibility and accomplishment. Do they feel challenged in their current responsibility level? Is there fair treatment and communication between employees and management? Are there certain perks that come with working in the environment or organization? These are some of the things that can enhance an employee's experience in the workplace. A box of donuts every now and then on Friday mornings doesn't hurt either.

Record Keeping—Managing employees means keeping track of their time and attendance and keeping an updated personnel file on all employees. Time and attendance is important to track for payroll purposes and for monitoring the use of sick or vacation time. Record keeping also includes notes and documents regarding employee performance issues, such as the time and date an incident occurred or a written warning to the employee for poor behavior. Keeping track of employee time, attendance and performance will help you assess their value to your department and to the organization.

Employee Performance Reviews—A major part of keeping track of employee performance is the performance evaluation. Many organizations set policies to conduct employee reviews on an annual basis. While the policy may differ from company to company regarding how and when, the process of conducting an official employee review should be consistent. Conducting reviews for employees should be timely, fair and constructive. The employee review process is such an important aspect of managing personnel, we will cover it in detail in Chapter 7.

Conflict Resolution—As long as there are at least two people in any given area, there will eventually be a disagreement between them. When managing multiple employees, there will be conflicts. As managers, we must mediate disputes and give fair judgment. Becoming involved in employee disputes is a requirement when managing personnel. It is important to listen to both sides of the story, get all of the facts regarding the dispute, and make a fair determination on the actions to be taken to settle the dispute.

Mentoring—Managing employees is about coaching and development. We discussed this earlier in this segment. Beyond coaching and development is mentorship. Managers must be a mentor to their subordinates and give them the proper guidance to succeed. Be the example you wish employees to follow and suggest ways they can improve their performance to gain future success.

Mentorship means providing the guidance and support to help an individual gain a greater understanding of what is necessary to succeed.

Discipline—When conflicts or non-conformances occur, it may be necessary to enforce corrective action upon an employee. Enforce discipline evenly among employees and document everything. There should be a code of discipline progression that allows a manager to ensure fair discipline standards. Depending on the severity of the employee behavior, a counseling session should be followed by a verbal warning and then a written warning. We will cover disciplinary actions in greater detail in Chapter 7.

These are the key areas of personnel management that must be managed. By understanding the role of the manager and what it involves concerning employee management, we can begin to develop key strategies to build relationships with our workforce. The better we manage these key areas, the greater we build the relationship with our workforce.

Servicing the Front Line Employees

The front line employees are the ones that are directly servicing the customers. They are on the front line of your business and a major reason for the success of the organization. Every job in every organization has, in some way or another, an effect on the front line employees. The role of the departments or business units that do not directly service the customer should be servicing those front line employees to create their ability to properly service the customer.

When servicing the customer, employees must be well trained and have the proper knowledge, tools and resources. One major resource for employees is their direct supervisor or manager. Therefore, the role of the manager is to service these employees to do their job. It is a reverse philosophy that states a manager must work for his employees rather than the employees work for the manager. When implementing this philosophy, the manager puts a strong focus on providing the employee the necessary tools, products, and knowledge to satisfy the customer requirements.

Servicing the front line employees means satisfying their requirements to perform their job.

Chapter Review:

Top reason why not to get promoted to manager: I will be accountable for everyone and everything

Managing Employee Checklist: Training, Coaching and Development, Scheduling, Delegation, Motivation, Record Keeping, Employee Performance Reviews, Conflict Resolutions, Mentoring, Discipline

Servicing the Front Line Employees: Satisfy employee requirements for them to do their job

CHAPTER 3

The Employee Focus

Managing in today's business has many challenges. As managers of a service area, department or business, we must balance our focus on four primary manageable areas. These four manageable areas are production, customer service, employees and cost. Depending on the size of the organization, these components may be managed by progressive levels of management. In either case, whether you are responsible for all four aspects or only a few of them, the key to overall business success is how well we manage the employees of the organization. Research has shown that the cost of labor is nearly 70% of the cost of doing business for companies from the very small to Fortune 500. When you think about it, that type of investment should be at the forefront of executive strategies to help achieve and exceed corporate goals and objectives. Managing employees, therefore, becomes the most important and subsequently most difficult of the four to manage. However, when managed properly, they will respond by managing the production and handling customer service for you.

> A well trained and motivated employee base will want to succeed and become part of the success of the organization.

A well trained and motivated employee base will want to succeed and become part of the success of the organization. This leads to increased productivity, greater care in the quality of the product, and a more positive approach to the customers who are receiving the product or service. The feeling of ownership by employees will ultimately help to control costs through a reduction in non-conformances and employee turnover, an increase in business interest from customers and an internal growth pattern that reduces the potential of high paid "Free Agents" to the organization. All of these results lead to a self-imposed control of operating costs which means a healthier profit margin.

The cost of employee turnover is rarely calculated into hard dollars. But when you analyze the loss of production from a well trained employee, the hard dollars and soft cost through time recruiting and hiring, the resources utilized to train and the decrease in employee morale due to a lack of a team environment, you begin to understand that controlling costs has plenty to do with retaining a good employee base. A well trained employee base can also eliminate costly production errors that can lead to the cost of reproducing the product or loss of customers due to a lack of confidence in the products the organization is providing. A well motivated staff is more prone to believe in the work that they are producing and care more about the customers that they are servicing. These philosophies, which have been proven in the business environment, lead to the realization that properly managing the employee base is a critical step towards managing the remaining three areas.

Understanding the Three Basic Needs

© From an article originally published in the September 2008 edition of Supervision Magazine

In any environment, the basic philosophy behind proper employee management is in the belief that employees have three basic needs to perform their jobs well. Employees must have the skills, tools and motivation to perform any job. These three basic needs are essential for any individual to be successful at an assigned task or responsibility. These basic needs are not, however, inherent in an employee. These basic needs must be provided during the employee's tenure with an organization. During that tenure, it is Management's role to supply these three basic needs for each employee. Management must ensure that these needs are consistently provided and that the employee becomes engaged in their role with the company. It isn't enough that an employee receives one or two of these needs.

The Three Basic Employee Needs

Skills - provided training to do the job
Tools - provided tools and proper equipment to do the job
Motivation - provided motivation and incentives to do the job

With over twenty-five years in the Mail and Office Services environment managing everything from print production and distribution to transportation, I have found that managing employees in the Office Services area does not have to be a difficult task when providing the production clerks with skills, tools and motivation.

Providing the employee with skills means being involved in the training process and allowing the employee to learn all aspects of the job. Training should be formalized with set goals to monitor skill development. A well developed training program with a focused trainer will give the employee the opportunity to acquire the technical knowledge and ability to perform assigned tasks. In the mail services environment, acquiring the necessary skills on mail sort techniques or mailing equipment becomes necessary for the employee to perform the job well. Proper training on specialty equipment such as an inserter or pallet jack can also reduce the risk of injury. Certification training such as fork lift operator or special Hazardous Materials Packaging can ensure proper procedures that limit risk and liability. Cross training employees for proper backup can increase their value and reduce headaches on the manager. It can even give the employee confidence in his ability to step up and solve problems in any service area. With the training program complete, the employee now has the technical skills to perform the job. But that is not enough for the employee to be effective.

We all heard the familiar phrase of having the tools of the trade. You can't build a house without a hammer and saw. Every employee must be provided the proper tools of the trade. Once again, in a business mail center environment, the office services clerk needs tools to perform certain functions of the job. The proper tools in any mail center can include updated address databases, either internally for mail sort or externally for mailing distributions. Upgraded technology and access to resources, even a well-organized mail cart for internal mail delivery sweeps, should be provided to maximize production performance. Management's responsibility to the employee is to provide adequate tools with updated technology in good working order. Much of today's stress in the business environment for a production employee is caused by inadequate or malfunctioning equipment.

This stress can be eliminated with the investment in the right technology and equipment to complete production and keep up with customer demands. A detailed analysis of the investment for new or upgraded equipment should include the functionality it lends to the production and the efficiencies it lends to the operation. Business trends continue to advance. Customers continue to expect more. Employees can be expected to maximize productivity with tools and equipment that is a right fit for the production environment. Without the proper tools, the employee cannot get the job done efficiently and effectively.

The third basic need for all employees is motivation. Employees must recognize that there is an incentive for performance. Motivation becomes the key ingredient in maximizing an employee's performance. Regardless of the skills and tools, if the employee does not have the incentives to perform the job, it will not get done effectively. Every employee is motivated in a different way. As managers, we are responsible for understanding what drives each employee and what management styles meet each individual's needs in order for them to become successful. Many times, it is not just the steady paycheck that drives employees to perform well. People need to feel a sense of gratification for what they do. Recognition and incentives for great performances are a few ways to keep employee morale high. Do they feel challenged to meet goals? What rewards are there for achieving goals? Is there fair treatment and communication between employees and management? Are there certain perks that come with working in the environment or organization? Many times, an open environment for communication can create a comfortable and relaxed working environment. These are just some of the things that can enhance an employee's experience in the workforce. Team spirit thrives in a high morale setting. Most importantly, Managers must become involved in the operation. People find it most comforting to work with a Manager rather than work for a Manager.

By providing these three basic needs to each employee, your work force will be better equipped to take on the challenges of any business. Further opportunities for career development can build an employee's interest in the company. With skills, tools and motivation, every employee on the team can respond positively in the workforce and put forth a great effort in achieving not only their goals, but company goals as well.

The Greatest Compliment

A manager is only as good as the employees he manages. To manage a process, you must first manage the people who handle the process. These statements are a good measuring stick to successful management. We cannot accomplish anything without having the right people doing the front line work. Therefore, it is great employees that make great managers.

This doesn't happen naturally, or completely on its own. To create great employees, we must manage them properly to make them great. That is what this book is all about. We can determine what makes a great employee. It is not just about production quality, but also about initiative, having a positive attitude, flexibility to changing environments, and overall attendance. It is easy to identify those employees. But managers are graded a bit differently. While those factors are important, managers have a different set of criteria in determining what makes them great. We will examine this further in the next chapter. For now, let's focus on a statement that can sum up what constitutes a great manager.

The greatest compliment we can receive as managers is that the successful advancement of our employees is a result of the coaching and development they've received from us. That is the true role of a manager. By coaching and mentoring employees to succeed, managers can build their reputation on how well their employees have advanced their skills and careers. In many organizations, this is the true measure of a manager's worth. If you are not training your employees to advance in their careers, they may never reach their potential. And if employees aren't reaching their potential, then they cannot be considered successful.

> The greatest compliment we can receive as managers is that the successful advancement of our employees is a result of the coaching and development they've received from us.

Employees who become successful due to the training and development they received from managers will build a great loyalty to that manager. Loyalty based on trust and respect is the greatest accomplishment. We will cover how we build this in the next chapter.

Employee Training and Development

Training and development is important at any stage of an employee's career. When it comes to technical skills and department processes, training and development is critical to establishing optimal performance from employees.

Training should be something that is scheduled and organized. All employees need training and development. Most training and development is handled from within departments and organizations. Training on specific job skills and company policies and procedures should be done directly. A well trained employee eliminates costly mistakes and increases knowledge, productivity and customer service.

One area of management under a Manager's responsibility is to manage production. When managing production, well trained and seasoned employees make this task simple. Employees should be trained on all aspects of production. These aspects include:

Technical Skills

Knowledge and Understanding of Equipment

Knowledge and Understanding of Products and Services

Knowledge and Understanding of Procedures

Setting Priorities

Meeting Deadlines

Quality Control

Time Management

Continuous Education

Continuous Improvement

The method of training in many situations should depend on the specific employee. Every employee must be seen as an individual. Because of this, managers must realize that each employee has a different learning method.

Some people may learn best from reading a manual and applying the acquired knowledge to the task at hand. Others may need to be shown step by step how to handle a process. Still others may throw the manual out the window and use the trial-and-error method, figuring out on their own what and how things work.

In every case, before starting a training session for an individual employee, the manager must first identify the employee's learning method. By understanding what best method works for the individual employee, a manager can adapt the training, development and coaching to the employee's learning method. This philosophy creates a more comfortable training environment and ensures a better learning experience for the employee.

Once employees are well trained in these aspects, a manager can begin to rely on the employees to manage their own production. Employees should be cross-trained in other responsibilities to become more valuable to the department or organization.

Training and development should not stop at the job function level. Further guidance and development should take place for employees to advance within the company or within their chosen industry. Training programs and opportunities should be available to all employees. Employees have an expectation from their manager and their organization to provide such training and development for their own career advancement. This training can include the following business functions:

- Customer Service—Customer service training should be a priority for any organization where employees are on the front line servicing the customer. This should include what the corporate policies are regarding customer service, how to handle difficult customers, and providing quality customer service relative to the industry. Customer service is the number one reason why customers build loyalty to a company. If your employees are not providing excellent customer service, they are not contributing to the success of the company.

- Product or Equipment Training—If your employees are responsible for the products or technical equipment within the department or organization, training on how to properly utilize these products or equipment should be administered. This includes training on products that are sold by the employee to better explain how these products can enhance the customer experience. Proper technical training for an employee operating machinery can eliminate costly production mistakes and even more costly injuries. Technical training for a sales force that is selling a product can be very helpful when explaining a product or answering questions from a prospective buyer.

- Sales and Marketing—Sales training is not just for those selling the products or services of the organization. Sales and marketing training can be a great benefit for anyone who comes in contact with the customer. Selling a product is not necessarily the object in many cases when dealing with customers. Employees must know how to sell the company. Employees must market the company and provide public relations whenever in contact with customers. Sales and Marketing training can enhance their ability to represent the company.

- Basic Supervision—Proper training should be provided for any employees who are ready to take a career step into supervision. This should include training on all the responsibilities that the employee will be expected to handle in the new position. Basic supervision training can be a part of the overall succession planning for a department or organization. If you are not thinking about succession planning for your department, you are not thinking about your own advancement. After all, someone needs to take your place when an opportunity for your advancement is available. By giving employees training for advancement opportunities, you are planning for your future as much as theirs.

- Certification Training—For employees who need certification for specific job functions, or can benefit from having a certification in a particular industry or business sector, training and preparation for the certification process should be provided. Certifications may be a requirement for specific jobs, such as Hazmat Certifications for shipping and receiving or CDL licensed drivers, forklift training for warehouse workers, or any other function that requires specific licenses. Other certifications can be obtained to provide credentials in an industry or a method of becoming a subject matter expert. This type of investment in employees gives you a more valuable and knowledgeable employee. More importantly, it builds their loyalty to you as a manager and the company.

Specific training on any area of needed development should be evaluated and provided as a way to improve employee potential. This can include communication skills, writing skills, or any personal development.

These are just some of the training sessions that should be offered to employees. Whether it is an in-house personnel training and development department or provided by external resources, training and development is a great way to motivate employees and give them the opportunities to succeed.

The Four Basic Employee Behaviors

Managing employee behaviors is a great challenge in today's society. There are many employee behaviors that are exhibited throughout a career, all which need proper management to control. Employee behaviors can be positive, negative, or indifferent. Human Resources techniques have been written and explained in numerous articles and books to deal with negative behaviors, but very few deal with positive behavior. This is because of a misguided conception that positive behavior does not need any control or management.

Whatever the behavior, managers must first identify the type of behavior before preparing any course of action. Employees, and individuals in general, can be categorized into four basic personalities. These personalities dictate the type of behavior. Below is an explanation of these four basic personalities.

a) Can-Will—This is an individual that has the necessary skills to perform the job and the proper motivation and initiative to perform the job.

b) Can't-Will—This is an individual that does not have the necessary skills to perform the job, but does have the motivation and desire to perform the job.

c) Can-Won't—This is an individual that has the necessary skills to perform the job, but does not have the motivation or desire to perform the job.

d) Can't-Won't—This is an individual that does not have the necessary skills to perform the job and no motivation or desire to try to perform the job.

As you can see from these four personalities, each has its own set of challenges. To better understand what necessary actions should be taken, we must first analyze why employees fall into these categories. We will start with the last personality, and subsequently the most difficult.

Can't-Won't—It may be obvious why this employee can't perform the tasks assigned. A lack of skills due to poor training or the lack of proper tools can certainly be an issue to getting the job done properly. (See Understanding the Three Basic Needs earlier in this chapter.) But what can explain the lack of motivation or desire? Perhaps the employee won't do the job because he can't. Fear of making mistakes is a great hindrance to initiative. Having the wrong tools, or the lack of tools, can also disengage employees from feeling compelled to perform. By providing proper training and the correct tools, the employee becomes capable of performing the tasks. This then changes the category of the employee to a Can-Won't employee or a Can-Will employee.

Can-Won't—What do you do when you have a skilled employee that just does not have the initiative or desire to perform the job? This is a challenging predicament for any manager because it becomes frustrating to know that the employee can achieve great success if he applies himself. A Can-Won't employee does not necessarily mean there is an issue with insubordination or an underperformance of job responsibilities. These are separate issues that need to be managed. Many times, a Can-Won't employee is someone who simply performs what he is assigned and nothing more than what he needs to do to get by. There is no initiative to expand his focus on other areas he is capable of handling. For a Can-Won't employee, managers must find out what reasons hinder his motivation. Perhaps the employee does not understand the reasons to perform other tasks, doesn't feel appreciated when performing other tasks, does not get recognition, or doesn't see any incentives or compensation for stepping outside his normal comfort routine. Proper motivation and communication tactics can help stimulate the employee into achieving a higher level of success. Recognition in a team environment and an overall understanding of team or department goals can help.

 Reasons for a Can-Won't Employee

Does not understand the reasons to perform other tasks
Doesn't feel appreciated when performing other tasks
Does not get recognition
Does not see any incentives or added compensation

Can't-Will—We've often heard statements from managers stating that getting the employee to show up for work is half the battle. So when we have an employee who has such a desire to perform, we should focus our attention on getting that employee all the skills and tools necessary for him to become successful. Unfortunately, when production errors do occur, it is usually met with disciplinary action without regard to analyzing the reasons for the error. When looking closely at an employee who has great initiative to do the job but lacks the productivity or quality, the first goal of the manager should be to build the employee skills through proper coaching and development rather than disciplining the employee through warnings and documented performance memos. Further training and a job assessment can give the employee a comfort level with acquired skills to minimize mistakes. Did the manager ensure that the employee's learning methods were considered during training? Is the employee ready for the level of responsibility necessary for the assigned job? These can be some of the reasons a Can't-Will employee would struggle with production performance.

Can-Will—Congratulations. You have a top notch employee. The Can-Will employee is a manager's best friend. He is the reliable worker who can handle any project and takes initiative to see it completed. He possesses great leadership qualities and can always be counted on when the pressure is turned up. As stated earlier in this section, there is a misguided conception that the Can-Will employee needs no management or course of action. It is common perception that the employee is empowered to handle projects and make decisions and will continue to maintain the status of a Can-Will personality. Nothing can be further from the truth. The fact of the matter is that a lack of managing this employee can lead to the employee feeling unappreciated and unchallenged in greater areas of responsibility. Without continuing to motivate, grant recognitions and mentorship towards a higher degree of success, this employee can easily slip into a Can-Won't personality.

By identifying the individual personality types for employee behavior, we can better manage each employee to perform up to and exceed expectations.

Chapter Review:

The Employee Focus: The cost of labor is nearly 70% of the cost of doing business

Understanding the Three Basic Needs: Give employees the skills, tools and motivation

The Greatest Compliment: The greatest compliment we can receive as managers is that the successful advancement of our employees is a result of the coaching and development they've received from us.

Employee Training and Development: Identify employee learning methods prior to conducting training sessions

The Four Basic Employee Behaviors: Can't/Wont, Can/Won't, Can't/Will, Can/Will

CHAPTER 4

Building the Manager/Employee Relationship

Management Development Progression Pattern Recap

The Management Development Progression Pattern was discussed in Chapter 1 to illustrate a necessary pattern for managers to follow in order to become successful in management. This progression pattern mostly pertains to the management of people.

To recap this progression pattern, here are the three progression steps that lead to management success.

1) Management Demands Leadership—You cannot be a great manager without first being a great leader.

2) Leadership Demands Discipline—You cannot be a great leader without first establishing great discipline.

3) Discipline Demands Character and Integrity—You cannot establish discipline without first building great character and integrity.

The most important point to realize with this progression pattern is that employees will recognize any break in this chain. In other words, employees will understand that without great character and integrity, a manager cannot have or enforce discipline, and so forth up the chain. The easiest way for a manager to gain the respect from employees is to build the relationship between manager and employee through this progression pattern. It certainly is not a quick or instant way of establishing management credibility, but it is the best and most lasting way. For managers who want to establish their credibility, taking the time to work their way through this progression pattern is well worth the time.

Employee Retention

The cost of employee turnover can be enormous and sometimes overlooked as a potential danger to productivity and customer service. Therefore, employee retention is an important responsibility and a worthwhile goal. Building a great relationship with employees can help retain good people.

Many companies subscribe to the philosophy of investing in the recruiting process to attract top talent. After all, finding the best people and bringing them into your organization is the first step towards building a successful team, and ultimately a successful business. This is a great philosophy to have, and if done right can indeed bring in top talent.

The challenge many companies face is not in attracting that top talent. It is in retaining it. Studies have shown that the cost of recruiting and hiring an employee is two times the cost of retaining current employees. It certainly is a cost advantage to keep good employees. And while cost in terms of dollars is an important aspect of this whole human resources responsibility, it is not necessarily the most important.

Creating a corporate culture that helps employee retention rates has far greater benefits than just the cost savings on the recruiting side for filling vacancies. Employees tend to stay with a company, even build loyalty to a company, when they feel that the company works towards efforts to retain top talent. Furthermore, it helps in building a reputation for the company when recruiting is done. Imagine being recruited by a company who has a passion for creating work environments that keep employees well motivated and engaged in their work. On the other hand, if that is not the case, and employee turnover is high, you may think twice about accepting that offer.

Reasons for Employee Turnover

In order to focus on employee retention, we must first analyze the reasons why employees may wish to leave a particular job. Many studies have been conducted to analyze reasons why employees leave their employment with a wide variety of results. Here is my list of top six reasons.

1) More Money—Money will forever be a motivator for many people. In some situations, a different career path may yield a better rate of pay. Other situations may see a competitive company willing to pay more to attract industry talent. In any case, employees may leave their current employment for more compensation.

2) Better Career Opportunities—Many employees have a desire to gain higher levels of responsibility, or just be interested in a different career industry that that which they currently hold. These opportunities may not exist now or in the future within their current employment. In these situations, it is hard to keep an employee who desires to take advantage of a career growth interest.

3) Conflict with Manager or Management—Employees can sometimes find it hard to adjust or adapt to a restrictive or dictating management style. Conflicts may occur between an employee and manager when there is no support or flexibility built into the relationship. Unresolved conflicts can lead to either resignations or terminations.

4) Workplace Environment—Some employees may have a desire or expectation to work in a business professional environment. Employees need to feel comfortable in their workplace and not be subjected to unprofessional habits such as poor dress code enforcement, use of foul language in the workplace, dirty and unkempt workspace, etc.

5) Lack of Teamwork—In any environment where there is more than one employee, teamwork is a necessary practice to motivate employees to achieve company or department objectives. Without teamwork, employees may feel unsupported, which can create a desire to leave their place of employment.

6) Poor Communication—One thing that can frustrate employees is a lack of communication. When employees are not informed of what is happening, or must wait days or weeks to obtain answers to questions only after asking three times, they lose confidence in the organization's management. This frustration can also lead them out the door.

This list is important to point out due to the overwhelming association each one has with the responsibility of management. Reviewing these top six reasons why employees leave their employment again with a management response will help to understand why it is important for a manager to focus attention.

1) More Money—Many managers have the responsibility of managing budgets. This falls under the managing cost category. While it is not practical to grant every employee a raise whenever they need it, it is a good idea to keep top performers properly compensated for their value. However, some employees, even the top performers at times, may find that they can work in a different industry and earn a higher hourly rate. When this happens, shake their hand and ensure that they leave on good terms.

2) Better Career Opportunities—Keep in mind that employees may just turn to a different career path and pursue an opportunity within their interested field. However, it is still important for a manager to understand that employee development is an important aspect of employee motivation. Management has the responsibility of developing employees to achieve success. When internal advancement opportunities become available, promoting employees who have taken the necessary development steps is a boost in morale for the entire department and entire organization. Better career opportunities can exist right within the company.

3) Conflict with Manager or Management—This is quite self-explanatory. If an employee leaves due to a conflict with the manager or management, the manager must first look in the mirror to determine what went wrong. Building great relationships with employees helps to avoid conflicts and keep employees happy and enthusiastic about their job. It is good to know that an employee can rely on the manager for the proper guidance and support and have the relationship that creates a comfortable working environment.

4) Workplace Environment—Continuing with the comfortable working environment, it is the manager that must create and control that environment. Setting the example is the first step towards creating a workplace environment. Correcting unprofessional behavior must take place to avoid the development of poor habits. A manager must be professional at all times and demand professionalism from their employees. A manager must ensure a clean and safe working environment.

5) Lack of Teamwork—Creating a team environment is a direct responsibility of a manager. A manager must put systems in place and have employees cross-trained to perform primary and secondary responsibilities. This give employees the ability to work and assist each other. The overall morale of the unit or organization depends on the teamwork environment that is created. Without this mentality, employees are left with a lack of support.

6) Poor Communication—Most often, communication that employees require or request comes from their direct supervisor or manager. If there are answers or information that employees are seeking that are beyond the manager's knowledge, it is imperative that the manager take ownership of the request to obtain the necessary information and communicate it back to the employee. Managers must also keep employees informed of everything relevant to their job. Without communication, employees cannot function properly.

Retaining top performers in an organization is critical to a business' success. By understanding these employee turnoffs that cause them to leave, and managing them, managers can have success in keeping a well motivated team.

Five Keys to Employee Retention

Managing the top six reasons for employee resignations is only half the battle. Now that we've analyzed why employees leave, we can focus next on what makes employees stay at a job. Studies have shown five key factors in employees willing to remain loyal to a company.

1) Job Satisfaction—Employees want to feel that their job is important to the overall success of the company. When employees feel appreciated for the job they do, and understand how that job affects the overall business outlook, they gain a sense of pride. This is a top

down philosophy that must respect employee positions at all levels. However, in many cases, senior management may not always be visible enough to show it. Therefore, immediate managers must make the effort to ensure job satisfaction for employees.

2) Development and Advancement Opportunities—Many employees will remain with a company if they see a career path. A company that is willing to invest in their employees will ultimately gain their loyalty. Many employees who see their jobs as career opportunities will stay at a company that offers development and advancement. Without it, they are destined to find that career path somewhere else. Managers should encourage employees to take advantage of development opportunities. If an employee sees you as an obstacle to their career goals, friction will soon follow. This will ultimately lead to an unwelcome separation.

3) Clear Expectations and Fair Performance Evaluations—Employees need to know what is expected of them and how well they are meeting those expectations. When expectations are understood, employees know how their performance measures up. In addition, there are no misunderstandings about job responsibilities that can cause confusion and frustration. Many companies require managers to perform annual evaluations. While these are a great way to provide constructive feedback, once per year is not enough for employees to feel engaged in their performance. Consistent feedback both positive and constructive is necessary to keep employees engaged in meeting expectations.

4) Incentives for Performance—Everyone likes to be rewarded for great performance. When companies add this philosophy to their corporate culture, everyone wins. Employees become more involved with the corporate culture and feel acceptance when their performance is appreciated and recognized. Many companies feel that in a tough economy, these type of incentive programs must be cut or downsized. What they fail to realize is that incentives do not have to be expensive. When companies make the effort to recognize their employees, even on a small basis, the effort usually goes appreciated by the employee. Programs like rewards for perfect attendance, On the Spot recognition awards, or even celebrating birthdays goes a long way towards employee job satisfaction. If a company does not have any programs, managers must develop their

own form of performance recognition to keep employee morale high. If you can't get corporate buy-in, don't be afraid to spend some of your own money. Just a simple $5 Starbucks Gift Card for a job well done can boost employee morale and gain a loyal employee. Now isn't that worth $5.00?

5) Fun Factor—The best advantage a manager or company can have is to make the work place an enjoyable place to work. Let's face it, no one wakes up in the morning jumping out of bed with tremendous excitement about going to work. What if we could make that happen? Maybe that's too high of an expectation, but you get the idea. Fun at work comes from having a great relationship with co-workers. Let employees laugh and build friendships. Organize fun events around Holidays or summer Fridays. Let's face it. Our lives can be stressful at times. So too can our work. Relieving that stress can be as simple as enjoying the time you are at work. Making the workplace a fun place to work can keep employees happy and motivated. Most importantly, it can keep them employed in your organization. And for your top performers, that is the entire goal.

 5 Keys to Employee Retention

Job satisfaction
Development and advancement opportunities
Clear expectations and fair employee evaluations
Incentives for performance
Fun factor

Building Trust Through Integrity

We learned from our Management Development Progression Pattern that the basis for all successful management is establishing Character and Integrity. Without these essential characteristics, a successful management of processes and employees cannot be achieved.

Building trust is a cornerstone to building great relationships with employees. Employees should trust that their manager will have their best interest in mind when making decisions, enforcing policy and resolving issues. This trust must be earned. Establishing and maintaining integrity is the key component for building that trust. If employees gain a sense that you have great character and integrity, they will form a trust in you and your ability to support and lead them.

There are three main ingredients to establish and maintain integrity.

 Three Main Ingredients to Establish and Maintain Integrity

Tell the truth
Act responsibly
Build solid character

1) Tell the truth—Always. Do not hide information unless it is truly confidential. And if it is confidential, do not hide behind a lie just to keep employees from asking questions. It only takes one lie to damage your reputation. Employees will forever remember that and hesitate to trust you again. Tell the truth and you will gain the respect necessary to keep your integrity.

2) Act Responsibly—Take responsibility for all your words and actions. Understand the consequences of each action and what effect it has on your reputation. Be responsible for everything that you control and people will begin to trust your judgment. This leads to further respect and trust.

3) Build Solid Character—The definition of Character, as defined by MSN Encarta is "the set of qualities that make somebody or something distinctive, especially somebody's qualities of mind and feeling." In other words, your character defines who you are. Character is created by the history of your actions. Therefore, to build solid character, your history of actions must be consistent with who you wish to be. Always tell the truth and always act responsibly, and a solid character will be built for you. Be cautious, as everything you do adds to that character. Do not create confusion by being inconsistent.

With these three guidelines in place, establishing and maintaining integrity can be achieved. Congratulations. You have passed the first stage of becoming a great manager.

Do What Is Right

We all learn right from wrong at a very early age. We learn that when we do wrong, there are punishing consequences for our actions. This is no different as an adult. When we do things the wrong way, things usually go wrong. People tend to remember what mistakes we have made far greater than what successes we've accomplished. That gives them a negative perception of us. Therefore, we must limit, or potentially eliminate, the amount of poor decisions we make. This is accomplished by following one simple rule. Do what is right all the time.

When we do what is right all the time, we build a reputation of being trustworthy. This further develops character and builds integrity. Doing what is right does not mean that we always have to be right. Sometimes, the decisions we make turn out to be wrong. This is inevitable. However, if the decision is made with the right intentions, we can survive the less-than-expected results. The more experience that is built by making decisions with good intentions, the greater the possibilities will be that those decisions will be the right one.

> When we do what is right all the time, we build a reputation of being trustworthy.

We all know right from wrong. We all know what intentions we have when we make decisions or actions. Do what is right all the time. Do not take short cuts. Do not use poor judgment. Do not cheat, steal or misrepresent anything. It is not good enough to do things right most of the time.

Employee Empowerment

The word empowerment means to grant authority. Employee empowerment is the practice of empowering employees to make decisions. Giving the authority to employees to act is a valuable business tool. This is such an important part of the management process that entire books have been written about the concept. There are many benefits to this practice.

Empowering employees to make decisions gives employees the feeling of involvement and ownership. Ownership tends to affect how people perceive their responsibility level. If granted the power to make decisions about their work, employees become compelled to do the right thing. Motivation and a sense of self worth increase. Experience and skill levels are advanced. A more productive and valuable team is created. Everybody wins.

Empowering employees to act and make decisions, however, is not just a simple policy to approve and implement with a wave of a hand. It takes management involvement to effectively administer the concept. Without an effective administration, employees will be prone to mistakes, a lack of confidence and unsure of how, when and what authority level they have. Implementing empowerment, therefore, takes time and patience.

Employees must be encouraged to make customer service decisions. This starts with a basic knowledge of what authority employees have when it comes to rules and policies. Employees need to know what rules can be stretched and what policies, under any circumstance, cannot be altered. Communicating the reasons for such can also give the employees a better perspective when it comes time to make decisions. Work with each employee to gain a sense of what their comfort level is about having certain authority. A common mistake when implementing this concept is the assumption that all employees will readily rise up and accept their new challenge. Forcing empowerment on employees who are not ready for this challenge may cause stress and a decline in their performance. Not many will have this problem, but few may. It may take more time or a different approach in these cases.

Employees must realize that with empowerment comes accountability. They will be responsible for their actions and decisions. As empowerment becomes greater, so does the responsibility level. As these levels grow, employees gain a sense of ownership. And when employees feel a sense of ownership, they are compelled to make better decisions.

Increasing employee empowerment creates a well motivated team of individuals that are capable of performing their job and building skills to take on the next job.

Qualities of a Good Manager

What has been covered in this chapter pertains to the relationship of the manager with the employee and how that can affect the manager's performance or image. There are many more qualities of a manager than just building relationships. Most of the qualities (if not all), however, provide the employees with a view and opinion of how good or bad the manager is at his responsibilities.

Employees will want managers to have certain qualities in order to gain their trust and respect. Below is a list of qualities that a good manager displays.

1) Provides a comfortable working environment. As stated earlier in this chapter, the manager is responsible and accountable for the environment of the workplace. By enforcing and maintaining a clean and comfortable working environment, employees can feel confident about their surroundings and about the person who is in charge of it.

2) Becomes involved and interacts with employees. Communication is good, but when it always comes from a memo or e-mail, the personal interaction becomes lost. Being involved and interacting with employees shows that you can support them and are a part of the team. Every manager should include a bit of the participating management style into their management traits.

3) Provides leadership through action. Leadership is built through a series of actions, not words. Pep-talks and motivational speeches are good, but without the actions to back those words up, the meaning and impact become weakened over time. Leaders show the way. They do not point to it for others to go forth.

4) Distributes tasks and discipline fairly. The key word in this quality is the word 'fairly'. Managers may need to manage employees differently, but they must be treated the same. Disciplining employees fairly also extends beyond treating employees the same. All employees may be reporting late to work, so if the manager does not address the issue with any of them, they are all being treated equally. But that is not necessarily being treated fairly. The manager must build the reputation of enforcing policy.

5) Acknowledges a job well done. Praise for good work is an easy motivator. Managers who understand this build positive relationships with their employees. Saying thank you to an employee for handling a special project or showing great customer service shows that you appreciate their efforts. If the employee knows it is appreciated, he will tend to repeat it.

6) Listens and responds to employee communications. One of the most frustrating things for an employee is when they communicate a question or concern to their manager and must continuously follow

up to get a response. Having good listening skills is important, but it becomes meaningless if there is no response or resolution to what has been said. Good managers listen, understand and communicate results back.

While not necessarily all inclusive, these six qualities are inherent in all good managers. By developing and displaying these qualities on a consistent basis, employees will respect the position and the person who holds it.

Qualities of a Great Manager

Displaying all of the above qualities is a good way to be respected as a manager. Why stop there? What turns good managers into great managers? Employees will look for certain qualities in a manager to gain their trust and loyalty to the organization. Below is a list of qualities that great managers display.

Please note that these qualities that make a great manager must also be preceded by the qualities of a good manager.

1) Knows and applies corporate policies. Managers of a department or sector of business must know and apply corporate policies. Managers must be a corporate resource for employees, as the manager is the first point of contact the employees have for such knowledge. Managers must be the corporate representative.

2) Develops a team approach to achieve corporate objectives. Once again, the corporate representative becomes important to establish the goals and build team unity in trying to achieve the corporate goals. Communicating this to employees is the first step in displaying this quality.

3) Is decisive and makes decisions with good judgment. Employees will begin to respect those managers who make decisions that produce positive and effective results. Many times, the employees expect that the position have the responsibility to make the difficult decisions, and that those decisions will turn out to be the right ones.

4) Provides development and mentorship for employees. A manager must train and develop employees to succeed in their positions. A great manager also develops employees to advance to the next

position. Providing this guidance and mentorship builds employee loyalty and an appreciation for the skills and advancement that is achieved.

5) Shows passion for the success of the employee and the success of the team. Managers expect employees to have a passion for their work. It all starts at the top. Managers must show the passion for creating a feeling of winning. They must show a passion for success, but not their own success. When employees see that passion, they feel compelled to succeed.

Once again, this list may not be all inclusive. However, every trait in both of these lists must be displayed to be perceived as a great manager. Just portraying a few, or perhaps just about all, is not enough. Employees will focus on the absence of these traits when forming opinions of their manager. Leave one out, and employees will notice.

Being a good manager takes simple steps and an approach to the team environment. Being a great manager takes the corporate approach while still maintaining the balance of corporate representative and employee support. Achieving that balance is the key to great management. The alternative should not be considered an option.

Consequences of a Bad Manager

So what is the alternative? Lacking the skills and traits of a great manager does have its consequences. The greater your management skills, the easier it becomes to manage your employees. Consequently, a lack of great management skills places the manager in situations that become difficult to control.

> A lack of great management skills places the manager in situations that become difficult to control.

Below is a list of employee traits that can develop over time from the lack of great management.

1) Low employee morale. Employee morale dictates the energy level in the workplace. A high morale means high energy and a willingness to perform. A low morale creates low energy and a lethargic

atmosphere conducive to a poor sense of responsibility. When poorly managed, employees tend to be less motivated to perform, which leads to a drop in morale.

2) Lack of productivity. Low morale leads to a lack of productivity. Employees lose their sense of pride for performance and begin to care less and less about the quality of their work. When poorly managed or improperly disciplined, employees have no motivation to succeed and perform well. This leads to production errors and non-conformances.

3) Poor customer service. When employees lack the focus or care of their work, and have low energy and low workplace morale, customers tend to notice. Customers need a friendly and comforting environment to be happy, and when that doesn't exist, there is already a negative tone set. Employees feed off the negative which results in applying that negative energy to servicing the customer.

4) Persistent unacceptable employee behavior. This can be as simple as tardiness or as difficult as attitude problems and confrontations with employees, customers or the manager. Unacceptable behavior can spread to the entire team when it is not dealt with properly. And when it is not dealt with properly, it escalates into even worse troubles for the manager. A poorly managed environment creates a poorly managed team. And a poorly managed team is impossible to manage.

5) High employee turnover rate. We can look back earlier in this chapter about employee retention. When employees leave, it creates work and a cost to recruit and train new employees. While the idea of trouble employees leaving may seem like an easy fix to the problem, the real problem lies with the management of the workplace. The new employee, no matter how highly motivated he is coming into the environment, will no doubt become a product of the environment. It is difficult to manage a team, or keep a team motivated, when the players constantly turn over.

6) Increased risk of legal liability. Some situations may lead to undesirable actions. Terminations can be legally disputed by the departing employee who feels he has been mistreated. Human Resources inquiries can stem from claims from employees against

the manager. Unemployment compensations can be awarded to departing employees with greater frequency, which increases costs to the organization. These are just some of the issues that can be faced when trouble employees are created by poor management.

As stated above, these consequences of poor management are not an option. To avoid dealing with these employee conflicts, refer back to the beginning of this chapter and begin to put the tips and guidance into practice.

Being a great manager takes time and patience. As discussed in chapter 1, management skills develop over time. There is no substitute for experience. As we gain the management experience, we become better and better at building these traits and making the right decisions. You will make mistakes along the way. Recover and move on.

The Bad Employee

In many employee management guides and expert opinions, they will want you to believe that there are no bad employees, only bad managers. This chapter tends to mimic that theory. We have been discussing the notion that portraying the management traits described builds a great team of great employees. While I tend to believe that this is true, there does have to be an exception to every rule.

The hard truth is that the bad employee does exist. Even in an environment thriving with great management and positive energy, there is the potential that one employee in the thousands that have been inspired by such management does not accept or respond positively. The best we can do as managers is to work towards a happy median that can be acceptable to both the manager and the employee. And when all possible tactics have been exhausted without compromise, it may just be that this individual is a bad employee.

In cases such as this, it is important to focus on how that employee can affect the rest of the team. Does the employee have any value or positive traits that contribute to the success of the team? Can that employee contribute without disrupting the positive energy and work environment? These are the questions that must be answered before deciding what to do. If there is no real advantage this employee brings to the team or organization, then isolate the poor behavior or work performance and begin to work towards a resolution, even if that resolution means termination. As managers, we do have the responsibility to make such decisions. While these decisions may be hard to carry out, they become important to maintain the integrity of the success you wish to accomplish with your team and your department. Deal with it properly and move on.

Chapter Review:

Employee Retention: Employees leave due to more money, better career opportunities, conflict with manager or management, workplace environment, lack of teamwork, poor communication

Build Trust Through Integrity: Tell the truth, Act responsibly, Build solid character

Do What is Right All The Time: Do not take short cuts. Do not use poor judgment. Do not cheat, steal or misrepresent anything

Employee Empowerment: Employee empowerment is the practice of empowering employees to make decisions

Qualities of a Good Manager: Provides a comfortable working environment, Becomes involved and interacts with employees, Provides leadership through action, Distributes tasks and discipline fairly, Acknowledges a job well done, Listens and responds to employee communications

Qualities of a Great Manager: Knows and applies corporate policies, Develops a team approach to achieve corporate objectives, Is decisive and makes decisions with good judgment, Provides development and mentorship for employees, Shows passion for the success of the employee and the success of the team

Consequences of a Bad Manager: Low employee morale, Lack of productivity, Poor customer service, Persistent unacceptable employee behavior, High employee turnover rate, Increased risk of legal liabilities

The Bad Employee: The hard truth is that the bad employee does exist

CHAPTER 5

The Four Steps to Gaining Respect

We discussed how building trust can gain respect from your peers and employees. Building character, maintaining integrity and doing what is right all the time will establish those qualities, which are necessary to successfully manage employees. But how exactly is this achieved? What actions must we take when managing employees to build that relationship?

Gaining respect is an important aspect of being accepted in any society. Likewise, that respect should be earned rather than forced or expected. Society tends to lean one way or the other in terms of establishing respect from others. In management, it is the same way. We either choose to respect someone for the position or power they hold, or respect someone for the words and actions they exhibit.

When respect is demanded from position or power, it usually is short-lived, or done so with apprehensive behaviors. In other words, saying "You need to respect me because I am the manager," may get you some respect. But this is demanding respect because you hold the title or power over those you manage. You may gain their respect, but you will not gain their trust. Nor have you developed any integrity that establishes your leadership skills. As we learned from our Management Progression Pattern, this will not work in building a positive working relationship with your employees. Therefore, holding the position of manager should not "entitle" you to respect from your employees. It should be earned in a way that makes employees choose to respect you as a manager, rather than having no other option.

The question still remains: How exactly is this achieved?

Character is defined as the distinctive qualities of a person that dictate predictable actions. It is the first step in the Management Progression Pattern, and it is no different in establishing respect. To build character, you must first establish a pattern of behavior. That pattern of behavior will ultimately define who you are as a manager. Once the character is established, it will determine whether or not employees respect you as a manager.

There are four distinctive actions that you can take in your management development that can help establish great character.

1. Focus on the good of the team

Making decisions is a major expectation and responsibility for managers. These decisions can be small, such as when to schedule lunch for an employee, or large such that it determines the course of business. From either extreme to everywhere in between, managers make decisions every day that affect the outcome of business.

When making decisions, managers must make all decisions based on the best interests of the team and the organization. Decisions must benefit the team and the organization, not the decision maker. This means that there should be no personal goals or gain. In other words: No personal agendas. Once a manager makes a decision that is perceived as making his job, and his job alone, easier, employees will lose respect for his ability to manage in a team concept.

2. Make sacrifices

Many experts agree that leadership starts with leading by example. Leading by example is the first step towards leadership, and a crucial part of the Management Progression Pattern. As a manager you must be the standard that you hold your employees to meet. Set the bar high and motivate your employees to reach that bar. Moreover, watch them reach beyond that bar. This is the result of setting the example and making sacrifices for your employees.

So what does making sacrifices mean? Show the team that you are willing to go the extra mile. If you expect your employees to work overtime when necessary, you must show that you are willing to put in the extra time as well. Sacrificing your time for the good of the project is setting the example. Managers who run out the door exactly at 5:00pm while their employees are busy figuring out how to finish the project by 5:30pm with equipment malfunctions will not earn great respect. Furthermore, employees will be less willing to go that extra mile for a manager who doesn't support them in times of need.

This is only one example of managers making sacrifices. A Human Resources friendly manager knows that sacrificing important labor hours for an employee who has a family emergency will result in great respect, and great loyalty. A family first approach is always a good philosophy. If it means you need to chip in with production, or delay the financial report you needed to complete, so be it.

It does not necessarily need to be a family emergency, but taking an interest and willingness to give employees flexibility will result in a return in flexibility when you need them. You won't need to remind them of the favor. They will return that favor willingly.

3. Communicate bad news timely and honestly

We learned in Chapter 4 that poor communication was a top reason why employees leave a company. Employees need information to function properly. Following through with this sounds like a simple thing to execute, and many managers do this well. So what is the issue?

This trait is not about communication. It is specifically about communicating bad news. Communicating and keeping employees informed is easy when it is good news, positive information, or simply industry or production topics that need to be discussed. But when it comes to bad news, we tend to become reluctant to discuss it.

There are several reasons why we are afraid to communicate bad news. 1) We are afraid of the reaction from the employee; 2) We are afraid to hurt the employee's feelings; 3) We are unsure of how to tell the employee, or when the best time is to tell the employee. These fears create a hesitation to communicate, and in many cases can create a lack of communication because the passage of time has made the news irrelevant. (But not unimportant.)

Communicating bad news timely and honestly is important to the employee. Employees may not like the news, but they will respect you for telling them.

Communicating the news in a constructive manner is also essential to gain respect. If there is an issue to discuss, reveal the issue, the reason for the issue and the honest forward progression to be expected. For example, if the company is expecting to downsize, discuss what you know and how it can affect your department and staff as early as possible. Most managers will fear that employee morale will diminish and employees will begin their exit strategy. Sure, this is a risk. But the entire concept of this book is to build employee relationships. If you have a great relationship with your employees, you will find that loyalty to you as a manager will override these risks in many cases.

The same concept of customer service applies to employee management. Feedback is important. Communicating bad news timely and honestly, without insulting or disrespecting the employee, is an important and essential skill to have.

4. Show compassion

Compassion is one of the greatest human characteristics. It can also be one of the greatest managerial characteristic. When things go wrong for an employee, whether it is in the professional life or personal life, showing compassion can build a human bond between a manager and an employee.

Compassion is a strong human emotion. We would no doubt show compassion for a friend who has suffered any type of distress in their personal life. As managers, we must realize that employees have a personal life outside of their work, and at times, life can be stressful. For this reason, be aware of external factors that may affect an employee's performance. Show that you care and provide good counsel if necessary.

I can't tell you how many times I've had employees, both male and female, begin to literally cry in my office. Whether it was of a personal nature or something on the job that they couldn't cope with at that moment, I gave them the opportunity to express their feelings. I've found it best to always have a box of tissues in my office. Offering a tissue to a teary eyed employee is a great way to show compassion.

A company that has a family first approach can gain great loyalty from employees. In the event where family matters dictate employee decisions, it should always be with a clear understanding that it is acceptable. This is, however, not without reason or boundaries. As employee behavior habits begin to form, there is a line between acceptable behavior regarding commitment to family and commitment to job responsibilities. However, when behavior warrants corrective action, it should not be without compassion. A good combination of concern for the employee welfare and for the employee's job performance is a delicate balance. Find that balance, and you will gain employee loyalty and respect.

Most importantly, when an employee's personal matters are discussed or when human emotions become delicate, these situations must be kept within your office walls.

Practicing these four behaviors as a manager can create trust and respect and build a great relationship for a manager and an employee. Once again, managers must display these behaviors all the time towards all employees. Being compassionate or making sacrifices some of the time and not for all employees can send mixed signals to employees about your character.

By displaying these four behaviors consistently, employees will be more willing to perform above expectations and put their efforts towards working for you. Plainly said, take care of your employees and they will take care of you.

Chapter Review:

The Four Steps to Gaining Respect: Focus on the good of the team, Make sacrifices, Communicating bad news, Show compassion

CHAPTER 6

Managing Employees Through Change

Change is inevitable. Change is also important. Continuous improvement in operations and technology will keep a successful organization ahead of its competition. Managers must realize that to be successful, we must initiate change and incorporate it into our knowledge-based skills.

Change can also be a frightful thing for employees. Change brings uncertainty. As stated, change is both inevitable and important. Just as important, however, is when and how the change occurs.

Process Change vs. Progress Change

There are two distinct forms of change in the business world. Each form is just as important as the other, but may be driven by different factors. It is important to know what factors dictate the form of change and when that change needs to be implemented.

Process Change is when any type of workflow or systems of processing is altered. These alterations are usually to enhance efficiencies, add accountabilities, or increase customer service. Changing the process of how we do things can be driven by competition and customer expectations or possibly by cost saving initiatives.

Progress Change is when any job responsibility or product is improved by technology or an increase in industry knowledge. This type of change is usually driven by innovative progress in engineering, technology, discovery or knowledge.

 Process Change vs Progress Change

Process Change - When any type of workflow or systems of processing is altered

Progress Change - When any job responsibility or product is improved by technology or increase in industry knowledge.

Let's take a look at an example in the photography industry to illustrate the difference between Process Change and Progress Change.

Linda, the owner of BrightColors Photo Developers, started her company with a small darkroom to develop film for the casual camera users. She promised her customers quality photographs that can be developed by the next day. She built a loyal customer base. To enhance her service, Linda decided to initiate a program where customers can drop off their film in the morning before 9:00 and pick it up in the evening after 5:00. This meant that she needed to either open earlier in the morning or establish a secure drop-off box at the door. She did both. Customers loved the new service. This is an example of Process Change. Linda changed the process of her workflow and service to give her customers a greater value.

Soon after that, Linda's customers began to use digital cameras. Digital photo processing did not require a dark room or chemicals. It required computer technology. Linda had a choice between acquiring new technology to meet her customer demands or gradually lose customers who no longer need traditional film developing. Linda decided to add computer processors and photo printers to be able to process digital photos from memory cards. She even established a website where customers can upload their photos for digital printing. This is an example of Progress Change. Because the casual photography industry had progressed from traditional film to digital images, Linda had to change the way she processed her work to keep up with the industry and remain in business.

Is Change Important Now?

After reading the example and explanations of change, we would all agree that change is an important part of a successful operation or business.

Without it, organizations would remain stagnant, falling behind competitors and customer expectations and eventually becoming obsolete. The one question that must be asked, however, is this: Is change important now?

The reason why this question must be asked is to evaluate the effects of change. Change may be perceived as good from an upper management perspective who ultimately can drive the change and enforce the change initiative. However, there are many aspects of change that must be addressed before proceeding. Change simply for the sake of change may sound like a good idea, but perceptions could rule out a favorable response. For instance, change to implement a Decision Maker's personal preference can be received as petty or unimportant to front line employees. If such is the case, these employees may not respond favorably to the change and cause resistance. The amount of resistance may be determined by how far removed the Decision Maker is from the employees and operation being affected, or by the distance in relationship of the Decision Maker from the employees.

By evaluating the reason for the change and how it will affect employees and the operation, we can determine whether or not the change is important to implement now. Sometimes, when the change is implemented is just as important as how and why.

Employees are key individuals in the implementation phase of any change. Employees are asked not only to implement, but positively sell the proposed change. Managers must build employee confidence in the change and get their buy-in for the involvement they will no doubt need to have. However, employees can be affected by the change in ways much closer to home.

Employee Fears

As stated earlier in this chapter, employees will be affected by the change simply because they will be the people who are asked to implement it. This creates a great workload for the employees, not to mention the education and training involved with the change that they must endure. But change can have a much greater, more personal effect on employees.

When change is discussed or considered, many fears initialize. The first question many employees will ask is how this change affects them, not necessarily their job.

1) Does it require new job skills?—The employee will want to know this. Some employees, and a great many of the long-tenured employees, may be fearful of learning new job skills, especially when new technology is introduced.

2) Does it mean a reduction in workforce?—Change based on a need to realign financial goals, but not exclusively because of this, could mean redesigning processes or eliminating waste to reduce the workforce. In cases of a decrease in production volumes may not necessarily lead to layoffs, but could potentially lead to reduced hours for the employees. This has a major effect on employees who rely on an hourly wage to support themselves and their families.

3) Does it require work shift changes?—Process changes could mean shift changes. Employees may be asked to change their shift from a daytime shift to a midday shift to accommodate the change. These shift changes could disrupt transportation schedules or family matters for the employee.

4) Does it mean greater responsibility for the employee?—There are some employees that do not crave greater responsibility. Career advancement does not appeal to everyone. Some changes may affect responsibility levels that are thrust upon them. Others may embrace the opportunities, while still others may be disappointed about not getting the opportunity.

5) Does it disrupt the space-time continuum thereby destroying the entire fabric of the universe?—Ok, this is quite extreme. No change implemented by a company (except that secret-secret project run by NASA) will have such an impact. So why bring it up? Believe it or not, there may be employee reactions to change that feel like such is the case. Managers must be aware of such feelings and manage change based on employee perceptions.

 **Employee Fears of Change**

Does it require new job skills?
Does it mean a reduction in work force?
Does it require work shift changes?
Does it mean greater responsibility for the employee?
Does it disrupt the space-time continuum?

These are the employee fears that must be considered whenever change is to be implemented. By managing these fears, change can be a comfortable and successful transition. Being empathetic towards employees who may have these fears will help them through the change process.

Communicating Change

Before any change is implemented, there must be clear and timely communication regarding the changes and how these changes will affect everyone involved.

From a personnel management perspective, staff meetings should be held on a regular basis. Staff meetings are a good way to keep communication flowing within the department and organization. It also gives an opportunity for employees to provide input, which can be very valuable when considering that they are on the front lines of any organization. Staff meetings should be held prior to any implemented change to provide instructions, support and comfort. These meetings may also provide valuable feedback from the employees as to how they can best work through the change.

Staff meeting should also be held during the transition to ensure that the change is taking the right course and having the right affect. It is also an opportunity to fix unforeseen problems that may occur during the transition. Lastly, staff meeting should be held after the transition to get feedback on the entire process.

Implementing Change

Implementing change can be exciting, confusing, terrifying or any other emotional feeling put into words. It all depends on perspective. One of the things we learn from managing employees is how each individual reacts differently to the same situation. Once we know how each individual will be affected by the change and what their reaction will be, we can manage each person through the change to make sure everything runs smoothly and everyone is comfortable about their own personal relationship to the change.

Implementing change should be the easy step if all the preparation stages have been successful. There should be an expected time frame to complete the change. Throughout the process, continuous evaluation and communication should take place to ensure that the change is being implemented properly and getting the desired results.

During the process, there may be several monkey wrenches thrown into the mix. No matter how well we prepare for change, unexpected things can pop up from anywhere that cause difficulties. Managers must stay involved in the entire process to handle the impromptu adjustments and keep all employees comfortable about the change decision. Without this involvement when things go wrong, the potential of losing the confidence of your employees becomes a concern. Rally the troops and move forward. Manage public relations to help your employees keep customers happy. Most of all, do not let the pressure of implementation cause you to revert back to old styles or processes. Remember why you made the decision to change and stick with it.

After the change is implemented, encourage feedback from everyone involved. Don't be afraid to make adjustments based on the feedback received. Sometimes, the results of change can be unexpected, whether good or bad. Celebrate the good and evaluate the bad. Lastly, be sure to thank those involved for creating a successful transition.

Chapter Review:

Understanding Process Change vs Progress Change

Is Change important now? Determine whether or not this is the best time for the desired change.

Employee Fears—Does it require new job skills? Does it mean a reduction in workforce? Does it require work shift changes? Does it mean greater responsibilities for the employee? Does it disrupt the space-time continuum thereby destroying the entire fabric of the universe? (A real concern.)

Communicating Change—Staff meetings are a great way to communicate with employees.

Implementing Change—Keep involvement from everyone and monitor the results of the change.

CHAPTER 7

Communication and Documentation

Communication is the key to success in any industry. It does not matter how much we know or how great our skills. The ability to communicate is essential to achieve any form of success in our career.

Having the confidence to communicate increases our ability to communicate. And when we speak with confidence, it builds confidence from those who listen. Develop these skills through public speaking exercises. The better you are at communicating, the greater your audience will respect your knowledge and position.

The Benefits of Communication

There are many benefits to great communication. It is a management tool that is often overlooked or underdeveloped. As in anything we want to learn and develop, communication skills are developed by continuing to communicate whenever there is the opportunity. Confidence is gained by increasing your development in the specific trait. Therefore, the only way to increase your confidence in communication is to increase your communication.

The three basic benefits of communication listed below can enhance our ability to manage production, customer service and employees.

Benefits of Communication

Prevent problems
Solve problems
Build relationships

Clear and proper communication has the ability to

1) Prevent Problems. When communication is clear and understood among all parties involved, the probability of errors is decreased dramatically. By having everyone on the team or who is involved understand the goal and how to achieve it, teams can work together to accomplish it. The ability to know when to ask questions for clarification and where to obtain information is also essential in preventing problems.

2) Solve Problems. When problems do occur, proper communication can help resolve the issues quickly and more accurately. Speak up and take ownership of the problem and do not hesitate to get others involved. Most problems can be solved with little or no ill consequences if communication is handled quickly and professionally. Do not waste communication on finding out who is at fault. Use communication to solve the problem and analyze the process to avoid future problems.

3) Build Relationships. The more we communicate, and the better we communicate, the greater respect we gain from those that we manage. This is the basis for building relationships. Always keep communication professional. It does not always have to be business, but it does always have to be proper. When you communicate, you represent who you are. If you are a business professional and you begin to use street language when discussing personal or current events, you begin to show a side that is not intended for your employee. Build relationships that you need in order to succeed.

Verbal Communication

Verbal communication, as stated above, is important to establish yourself as a business professional. To succeed with verbal communication, it is necessary to understanding the many aspects of it.

Many studies have shown that the effectiveness of face to face communication requires both verbal and non-verbal aspects. Most people listen at 25% capacity and tune out 75% of what is said. Even more interesting is that the spoken word only accounts for 7% of face to face communication. The remaining 93% is non-verbal. This includes tone and expressions.

We need to keep these statistics in mind when conducting any form of verbal communication. In order for the listener to completely understand what is said, we must communicate properly to ensure that the message is clear. Here is a list of things to consider when conducting verbal communication.

1) Tone—The type of tone we use when communicating can have a varying degree of effectiveness to the listener. The tone of our message should match the desired effectiveness we what for our message. For example, if you are communicating to provide information, the tone should be calm and straightforward. If you are communicating guidance instructions, the tone should be reassuring. And if you are communicating discipline or a stern warning, the tone should be stern and commanding. Either way, the tone of the message ensures that the message is received with the proper desired effect. Otherwise, the message may not be as clear.

2) Selected Audience—It is always a good idea to know who the audience is when delivering your message. Is the message intended for the particular audience or should it be directed to someone else? Is the message appropriate for the selected audience? Will they understand the message? For example, an auto salesman needs to know what the buyer is really looking for in an automobile before he delivers his sales pitch.

3) Non-verbal Feedback—Looking for feedback from the listener is a good communication practice. Look for signs that the recipient of your message is grasping your message. If not, you may need to change the delivery method.

4) Verbal Feedback—Allow for the recipient of the message to respond and ask questions. This is a good way for the listener to ensure he received the proper message. Do not always assume that the message is clear and understood just because you understand it. Allow for

conversation, even if it is slightly off topic. Respect the listener's point of view.

Verbal communication is essential to keep business relationships alive. When done properly and professionally, it can be a useful tool in managing people and processes.

Communication Philosophy

In today's electronic world, email communication has become a popular and widely accepted form of business communication. More and more business communication is being done via email.

The one problem in today's business society, however, is that email is seen as a form of escape from proper communication. Building relationships has always been done through interaction with the individual. The better we know and understand that individual, the better the relationship will be. With that said, it is nearly impossible to know and understand an individual strictly through email communication.

> It is nearly impossible to know and understand an individual strictly through email communication.

With that said, Email communication does have its advantages over other conventional methods. Email can be useful for the simple or complex transfer of information. Need to send someone information? Just type up an email, or send an attached file, and press send. The recipient gets what he needs fast and is probably happy about it. Email is also a useful time management tool. Rather than printing out a document and sending it in the mail, or spending time over the phone chatting about so many off-topic subjects, an email is quick and painless and keeps you focused on your other tasks.

There are also some disadvantages to the simplicity of email communication that also bear noting. As stated earlier in this chapter, communication is 93% non-verbal. Things like tone and expression are completely lost in an email communication. An email to an employee that reads, "I noticed you showed up late yesterday" could have many different meanings. Is the sender expressing his displeasure with the fact that the employee showed up late? Or could it be just a concern about the employee's well being? Is it a message that you are watching this employee and he had better straighten up his act?

There are a lot of interpretations that are left for the recipient to decipher, and often times that interpretation is wrong. Do not leave interpretation of your message to chance. Avoid email communication when the tone of the message is important.

Email communication is also an easy way out of communicating bad news. Too often, managers like to hide behind emails to convey a strong disciplinary message. Today, some experts may say that this is a great way to communicate these situations because it automatically documents the message. However, what it does not do is build the relationship and respect for the sender, something that is equally important. Face to face communication continues to be the most effective way of delivering a message when the relationship is important. A follow up email is a good idea if you want to reaffirm or document the message.

A simple rule to follow for this philosophy is this:

- For information sharing: Email is a great tool.

- For problem solving: Telephone or face-to-face communication is recommended. Email is a great confirmation follow up.

- Relationship building: Telephone or face-to-face communication is necessary. Email is a great tool to bridge the gaps.

Managers that communicate to employees strictly through email tend to lose the personal touch and relationship with those employees. For those managers who manage off site employees, or employees who work in virtual offices, these rules still apply. Maintaining a personal touch reaffirms the relationship and builds respect.

Disciplinary Documentation

Whenever you are managing employees, it will become necessary in the course of that management to enact disciplinary measures. When conducting disciplinary action, whether it is a first time verbal conversation to correct an issue or a stern final warning, it is important to document the action.

Disciplinary documentation is essential for when determinations on corrective action are to take place. Many organizations filter severe actions, such as suspensions or terminations, through the Human Resources

Department. This is because Human Resources Specialists know how to protect the organization against liabilities from disciplinary action. Proper documentation prior to any severe action is a way of protecting the organization.

Proper documentation could mean the difference between winning or losing an unemployment hearing when the terminated employee tries to collect unemployment compensation from the State. The burden of proof always lies with the employer to show just cause for the termination. Proper documentation protects the employer and is the proof of justification. It could also protect against more serious conditions that a terminated employee may wish to pursue, such as an Equal Employment Opportunity Commission complaint or a lawsuit against wrongful terminations.

Documenting disciplinary actions can be a simple memo to the employee file noting that a meeting took place or a written warning that requires an employee signature confirming that the employee received and understood the contents of the written warning. Whatever the case, the document should be brief and state clearly the facts involved. Below is a guideline for what should be included with such documents.

- Date and Time of the Disciplinary Action. State when the action took place.

- Who was Involved. State all parties involved with the action and what their position is with the company.

- Reason for the Action. State why the action is taking place by using specific details regarding the employee's actions that caused the discipline. If dates are involved, such as a trend of tardiness, list all dates the employee was tardy or displayed the unacceptable behavior.

- Consequences. State what the consequences could be if improvement of the behavior is not made.

- Employee Signature. If this is a written warning, get the employee to sign the document acknowledging that the warning was discussed with him. Note: Managers do not have the power to force a signature from the employee. If the employee refuses to sign, make a note on the document that such was the case. Do not threaten the employee for not signing a document.

If the document is a final warning, the consequences of continued unacceptable behavior must be clearly written. A common phrase used in most final warning documents is "further unacceptable behavior of this nature may result in further disciplinary action up to and including termination." This clearly indicates to the employee that they can be terminated if no improvements are made within a reasonable timeframe. That timeframe may even be spelled out in the document. Once again, this can protect the organization against any retaliation from the employee if a termination is the result of future repeat behaviors.

The practice of documenting employee behaviors and disciplinary actions makes it easier for the organization to take severe action when necessary. Many Human Resources Departments within an organization may not carry out terminations if the proper documents do not support the action. Of course, there are varying degrees of behavior that may warrant immediate termination. Office violence and theft may be a few. In these situations where the employee is justifiably terminated immediately upon the behavior, it is still important to document the employee file as to what took place using the guidelines above.

> The practice of documenting employee behavior and disciplinary actions makes it easier for the organization to take severe action when necessary.

The best practice is to document everything. A common phrase in the management world is, "If it is not documented, it did not happen."

Writing Employee Evaluations

The employee evaluation process can be a stressful process for a manager and sometimes for the employee. But it is a necessary process for any organization to conduct a periodic review of the employee's performance, even if there is no pay rate increase involved. Many companies have implemented a process where new employees are evaluated after 90 days of working at their new job and all employees once per year. This is a good policy to have.

Conducting an employee review begins with writing the report. Many companies provide a specific Review Form to be used. However, if a specific form is not available or used by the organization, a written document listing each job function and a performance rating for that function should be manufactured. Also, general Employee Review Forms can be purchased from various HR sources as well as some Office Suppliers such as Office Depot or Staples. It is important to keep all employee reviews consistent with each other to ensure that all employees are being evaluated on the same level, function and performance expectations.

In writing an employee review, the following guide can help create a professional and informative document.

1) Evaluations should be typed. In today's electronic world, even paper forms can be transitioned into live electronic documents. A typed review establishes the professionalism of you and the company you represent.

2) Proof for spelling and grammar. Use proper grammar and check spelling. Poor spelling and grammar diminishes the image of your qualifications to be conducting an employee review.

3) Direct the review to the recipient. Do not use "he" or "she" in the review. Write the review as if you are writing to the employee. Make the review personalized by addressing the employee.

4) Be direct and give specific examples of how you've come to your decisions on performance. As a manager, you should keep in mind everything during the review period that the employee accomplished or failed to accomplish. Write the specifics in the document.

5) Give compliments where appropriate. If the employee has done a great job in one area or function, it is always nice to compliment the employee on the review document. "Thank you for your great efforts in this area," is a good closing sentence if it is well deserved.

6) Give proper constructive guidance where necessary. If the employee is not performing up to expectations in one area or function, document what the employee can do to improve.

7) Numeric ratings should match the comments. If your review process involves a numeric grade, make sure that your written comments match what grade you have given. If comments do not match the rating, it can create confusion or misunderstanding from the employee's perspective regarding his performance.

When writing an employee review, it is also important to know what NOT to have in writing. The following list should guide you in what should not be included in a written employee review.

1) Do not offer compliments of a personal nature. As stated in point #5 above, giving compliments where appropriate is a good idea. But stay away from complimenting any employee on a personal nature, such as stating that the employee "has a pleasant smile". Evaluations are based on business performance and not personality or personal attributes.

2) Do not make specific recommendations for promotions. Making recommendations for further advancement for the employee, especially when you as the manager do not control such decisions, can give the employee a false promise of advancement.

3) Do not use the phrases "I think", "I believe" or "I feel" to begin a sentence. These phrases generally give the connotation that you are forming an opinion. Your evaluation should be more direct and not be up for interpretation or objectiveness.

4) Do not leave any area blank. This gives the impression that you did not take the time to evaluate these functions or skills. If the function or skill does not apply, document why and what the intentions are to get the employee these skills.

5) Do not compare the employee to any other. If you need to make a comparison, compare the performance to what the expected standard performance level is and not to what anyone else in the department or organization has done.

6) Do not provide disciplinary documentation or final warnings. If there are performances that are below expectations and deserve disciplinary documentation or actions, it should be done in a separate document and a separate meeting. The review process is simply a review of performance. Include past disciplinary actions as examples, but do not use the written evaluation or review process to conduct disciplinary action.

7) No surprises. Employee reviews are just that. A review of past performance. Unless a particular action took place just prior to the

review leaving no time to discuss it beforehand, there should be nothing noted in the review that the employee hasn't already heard throughout the course of the tenure. If an employee performed under expectations for an entire year, now is not the time to suddenly bring up all the non-conformances. Make sure the documentation is consistent with any previous feedback that was given the employee during the course of the employment period.

Once the review is written, read it to yourself to ensure that all areas have been completed and all spelling and grammar is correct. Do not be afraid to solicit feedback from your manager or a Human Resources representative to get a second opinion on the document. While no one may know the performance of the employee better than you, someone else with proper authority to review the document may have valuable input in how it is written.

Conducting Employee Evaluations

Once the employee evaluation is written, it is then time to meet with the employee to review the performance. Most employees look forward to their reviews and know when it is time for the review to be conducted. For this reason, it is a common courtesy to conduct the review timely. If the review process is to be delayed, inform the employee what is causing the delay and give the employee a reasonable time you will be able to complete the process. This will give the employee the feeling that you do understand its importance and that you want to take the time to conduct the review properly and with the correct attention.

Many employees may feel stress due to the fear of how their performance will be evaluated by their manager. Other employees may want to prepare themselves for the review meeting to discuss their own evaluation of their performance. This is perfectly acceptable. For these reasons, the review meeting should be scheduled and performed in a private setting such as a closed office or a conference room. Enough time should be allotted to conduct the review and allow the employee to give feedback and responses. Do not allow for the review process to feel rushed, as this can diminish the effect and perception of its importance. Do not allow for interruptions during the review process and make every attempt to conduct the review as scheduled.

Make sure that you are prepared to conduct the review. Most positive reviews are easy to conduct. But when employee reviews include some areas of improvement you wish to express, it takes time to prepare for how you present this and how you respond to any adverse reaction from the employee. Always be prepared to defend your evaluation of each category and function. In many cases, documented examples will help. Be prepared to provide advice as to how the employee may improve in areas where his performance was below expectations.

When conducting the review, make the employee feel comfortable. Employee reviews are meant to be constructive. A comfortable setting and a positive start will let the employee know that the entire process is meant to be a forward step in the employee's development.

> Employee reviews are meant to be constructive. A comfortable setting and a positive start will let the employee know that the entire process is meant to be a forward step in the employee's development.

Do not just read the evaluation document to the employee. The employee should be given the opportunity to read it, but it is best if you as the manager discuss the review rather than read it. Encourage feedback from the employee, even if that feedback is contradictive to your evaluation of the performance. Understand that no employee likes to be told they are not performing up to expectations. Respect their opinion, but stand firm with your evaluation. If the employee brings a valid point to the table that you may have overlooked, don't be afraid to acknowledge it and thank him for bringing it to your attention. If there is to be an increase in pay, explain the factors that determined what the increase is to be.

Lastly, end the review meeting on a positive note. The goal of an employee evaluation is to make the employee feel confident about moving forward with the company. Thank the employee for the time and effort put forth into the organization and offer continued guidance and assistance to his career.

Chapter Review:

The Benefits of Communication—Prevent problems, Resolve problems, Build relationships.

Verbal Communication—The spoken word only accounts for 7% of face to face communication. The remaining 93% is non-verbal.

Communication Philosophy—For information sharing, email is a great tool. For problem solving, telephone or face-to-face communication is recommended. For relationship building, telephone or face-to-face communication is necessary.

Disciplinary Documentation—If it is not documented, it did not happen.

Writing Employee Evaluations—Proof for spelling and grammar, Direct the review to the recipient, Be direct and give specific examples, Give compliments where appropriate, Give proper constructive guidance where necessary.

Conducting Employee Evaluations—Employee reviews are meant to be constructive.

CHAPTER 8

Human Resources

As we discussed in chapter 2, having the title of Manager has a great responsibility to the organization. As a manager, you are a part of the management group and represent the organization from a management perspective. Because of this, human resources is a vital part of the management skills. Many organizations will have a central Human Resources Department to handle corporate human resources objectives. But as a manager of a department or sector of business, it is your responsibility to maintain and carry out human resources responsibilities. As a manager, you are accountable for your actions, including any human resources related actions and issues that you may face. Be prepared to deal with these issues properly. Otherwise, you and your organization can be in danger of human resources liabilities.

Benefits and Compensation

Many companies provide benefits to their employees such as health insurance, retirement plans and other forms of family and wellness plans. As a manager of employees, it is a good tip to understand these company benefits and to be a front-line resource. While many department managers are not expected to know the explicit details of the health plans and other benefits that the company can provide, employees will still look to the manager to assist and direct them in the right way.

Companies also will offer employees personal time off (many times referred to as PTO) in the form of vacation time and/or sick time. Managers are responsible for tracking this time and keeping accurate records of how much time each employee has accrued, when employees have used vacation or sick time and any balance of time the employee has left to use. It is important to know and understand the company policy regarding accrual and usage of such time.

Compensation generally refers to the hourly rate of pay or annual salary that employees earn. Compensation also includes any commission based pay. Many managers are responsible for setting these pay rates. With this responsibility comes a fiscal responsibility to the organization. Employee pay rates directly affect the organization's operating costs. Many organizations will set pay scales for positions based on job descriptions of each position. If such is the case, know what those pay scales are for each employee you manage and where they fall currently on that scale.

Another fiscal responsibility regarding pay rates is controlling overtime costs. When employees work overtime, it can be a costly option for the company, generally paying employees at time and a half their pay rate. A manager should monitor work hours to ensure that overtime is worked only when necessary. A good policy is to have overtime hours worked only upon approval from a supervisory level. When work hours are not monitored and controlled, employees may take advantage of opportunities to earn extra pay that could cost the company unwanted expenses. And when that happens, it becomes a poor reflection on the manager's ability to control labor costs.

Motivation and Job Performance Incentives

All of the principles and philosophies discussed in this book centered around managing employees. By putting these principles into practice, you are well on your way to properly motivating your employees. A well managed employee is a happy employee, and a happy employee is easy to motivate.

> A well managed employee is a happy employee, and a happy employee is easy to motivate.

Employees find it easy to work in an environment free of stress and confusion. While we may not be able to eliminate the stress caused by heavy workloads or demanding customers, a manager can help support employees in handling the stress levels. Don't be afraid to invite some fun into the office. Allow personal conversation within the office as long as it does not interfere with production, customer service, or unwelcome topics. (The three biggest topics to avoid in the workplace are Sex, Religion and Politics.) Celebrate birthdays or individual accomplishments. Thank employees and provide recognition when they have produced outstanding results.

When a manager genuinely shows appreciation to an employee for a job well done, it compels the employee to achieve greater success. Find ways to award success, no matter how small or silly it may seem. Adding these motivational tactics and incentives creates a competitively fun environment for the entire team. A popular management phrase is, "Getting the employee to show up to work is half the battle." When you make the workplace environment a fun place to be, employees will feel good about coming in to work. Consider half the battle already won.

Harassment and Other Workplace Issues

Harassment in the workplace is a common and serious issue. Many people associate harassment with the most common form, sexual harassment. However, harassment can be in many other forms, such as ethnic harassment and bashing or bullying individuals based on their appearance or personality. This is illegal in the workplace and must be controlled by the manager.

The most widely accepted definition of Sexual Harassment comes from the Equal Employment Opportunity Commission (EEOC). The EEOC defines Sexual Harassment as:

The unwelcome sexual advances, requests for sexual favors and/or other verbal or physical conduct of a sexual nature when submission to such conduct: a) is implicitly or explicitly a term or condition of an individual's employment or basis of employment decisions; b) has the purpose or effect of unreasonably interfering with an individual's work performance; c) has the purpose or effect of creating an intimidating, hostile or offensive work environment.

There are two forms of sexual harassment defined in the legal industry:

1) Quid pro quo is a Latin term meaning "this for that". It is the action of granting a privilege to someone based on that individual performing a sexual favor. An example of quid pro quo is when an

employee is denied a promotion or a requested vacation day because he/she refuses to be romantically involved with his/her supervisor. Another example is when an employee is treated unfairly or disciplined unfairly because of the same reasons.

2) A Hostile Environment is created when there is unwelcome behavior, whether sexual or not, and/or behavior that creates a hostile or intimidating environment A hostile environment is recognized by the individual or individuals who have directly or indirectly experienced the unwelcome behavior. This means that the behavior does not necessarily have to be targeted towards the individual who feels intimidated or uncomfortable about the behavior.

Hostile Environment

The most common form of harassment is in the creation of a hostile environment. An environment is considered hostile when it creates an intimidating, hostile, abusive or offensive environment. Behaviors that can cause a hostile environment include:

- Unwelcome sexual remarks, jokes or taunting

- Displaying of graphic descriptions of pornography

- Repeated requests for dates

- Demands or requests for sexual favors

- Unnecessary touching, grabbing, patting etc.

- Leering or suggestive gestures

- Utilizing terms of endearment (Sweety, Honey etc)

- Obscene phone calls

- Unwanted e-mails or letters

- Public Humiliation

- Bashing due to sexual orientation, ethnicity, personal appearance or personality

- Forcing a kiss

A hostile environment is created when one or more of these behaviors are repeated. The key to controlling the environment for a manager is to educate employees on the subject of unwelcome behaviors. These behaviors are less likely to occur when all employees understand the seriousness and consequences these behaviors cause in the workplace.

When an occurrence does happen, the manager must respond immediately. Most organizations will have the manager report such behaviors to the Corporate Human Resources Department or a Senior Representative that has Human Resources responsibilities. Be sure to strictly follow the guidelines set by your organization. If not, the consequences of a poor response to these behaviors could rest on you as the manager.

Most often, harassment situations can be resolved through communication. Meeting with the victim to gather the complaint is always the first step. Meeting with the accused to discuss the allegations naturally would come next. Usually, getting the employee to understand the seriousness of the alleged actions and proper guidance moving forward can resolve the situation. If not, further involvement from a Human Resources professional is necessary. Managers without experience in dealing with these issues should immediately get a Human Resources Representative involved prior to initiating any form of investigation or communication.

Even if the first encounter is quickly and satisfactorily resolved, documenting the incident is critical. As we discussed in chapter 8, documenting everything is a great management practice. In harassment situations, consider it a mandatory action. Documenting these situations with a memo to a Human Resources professional signifies that you have done your job by getting actively involved immediately and have notified the proper personnel. This is important if future occurrences should happen. Remember that you are accountable for everything that happens within the scope of what you manage. Therefore, consider your job on the line if harassment situations aren't dealt with properly.

Violence in the workplace should be handled in much the same manner. Education on the subject of violence in the workplace can eliminate any threat. However, there can be an occasional argument between employees every now and then. When this occurs, the manager must step in immediately to avoid any further escalation of the argument that could lead to violence.

While harassment may not be an immediate terminable offense, severe violence can result in immediate termination. The workplace is no place for street brawls or fisticuffs and is a poor representation of the professional standards that must be kept.

Make note of all relevant information when documenting harassment and violence incidents. This should include the date and time of the incident, the people involved in the incident, the people who witnessed the incident, words and phrases that were used during the incident, and your response to the incident.

Many times, unwelcome behavior exists because one individual does not consider the action inappropriate. Education on what is and is not appropriate, and setting standards on such behavior, can eliminate the subjective views of certain behaviors. A good rule to follow is, "If you think it may be inappropriate, consider it inappropriate."

> If you think it may be inappropriate, consider it inappropriate.

The best way to avoid harassment and workplace violence situations is to maintain a positive and professional workplace environment at all times. Educate employees on the danger signs and correct problems immediately. Most often, harassment and violence stems from repeated behaviors that go uncorrected. Do not let these behaviors escalate. Lead by example and enforce professionalism and respect among co-workers.

The Human Resources Department and the company's Legal representative can and should provide further training and assistance to deal with such issues. Reach out to these resources.

Safety and Security

In chapter 2, we discussed the number one reason why not to become a manager. To review, that reason was: "I will be accountable for everyone and everything." This is a scary aspect of management when it comes to safety and security.

Safety and security is everyone's responsibility. When guidelines are established to ensure the safety and security of the workplace, the potential for hazards is greatly reduced. A manager of a department and employees is directly responsible for the safety and security of everything under his management.

Below is a guide to maintaining a safe and secure work environment

1) Limit access to the workplace and workstations—Work areas that have easy access are prime targets for suspicious visitors and behavior. Limit the access to your department to essential or welcomed personnel and visitors.

2) Secure all entrance ways to company premises—If your department has access to the exterior, such as a building community hallway or the outside world, make sure the entrance way is locked and secured at all times. Unsecured entrance ways to the company can be accessed by anyone, and can be accessed unnoticed during some periods of the work day.

3) Keep loading docks properly staffed during business hours—Loading docks are prime entrance ways for unwelcome guests. Many times, valuable materials may be left on a dock waiting for pick up or delivery. These items can disappear quickly if the dock is left unattended and unsecured.

4) Have a secure place for employee belongings—Even if your workplace is secure from intruders, be aware of internal thefts that could occur. Do not allow employees to keep their personal belongings out in the open. This invites the opportunity for theft.

5) Identify all guests and unfamiliar visitors—Be sure that you know who is entering your department and for what purpose. Approach and question anyone unfamiliar to you or your staff. It is easy to spot someone who looks suspiciously out of place. Be aware of those who try to get in by playing smooth and inconspicuous.

6) Identify all mail and packages that pass through the department— Mail Center Security is a hot topic. Suspicious packages should be intercepted immediately by Mail Personnel. But don't always assume that an item passed through their inspection. Identify all packages and the delivery method.

These helpful tips can keep the workplace safe from crime and damage. But when discussing workplace safety and security, it is also important to focus on safety from workplace injuries.

Below is a guide to maintaining a safe environment to avoid workplace injuries

1) Keep office equipment properly maintained—If your staff operates machinery or office equipment, be sure that the equipment is functioning properly. Injury can be caused by machine malfunction or by employees trying to fix the problem themselves without the proper technical training. Avoid these situations.

2) Keep office floors and walkways clear of objects and debris—Injuries can occur when employees trip over boxes or cables and wires that are left in heavy traffic areas. Doorways should be clear for easy access. Hallways should have the maximum recommended clearance for safe passage.

3) Limit the height of stacked boxes and items—Keep a limit to the height of stacked boxes and items to avoid tumbling. If the top box or item in a stacked pile cannot be reached without stretching, or if the top items are leaning in any direction, consider the stack height too high.

4) Keep the office well illuminated—Replace burnt out light bulbs immediately. Proper lighting can avoid mishaps and strain on the eyes. If all lights are functional and there is still a sense of darkness, consider other sources of light, such as desk lamps. Also, do not hesitate to speak to the building facilities maintenance to create more light.

5) Ensure that all relevant materials and supplies are within reasonable reach—Having commonly used supplies and materials within a safe reaching distance can eliminate costly injuries. Be careful not to

stack supplies too high on shelving where they are difficult to get. This creates a risk of pulling a muscle or an event of a falling object. Ergonomics should be considered when laying out storage of supplies and office space.

These tips can help provide a safe working environment for your employees. For more information on workplace health and safety, you can visit the US Department of Labor Occupational Safety and Health Administration (OSHA) website at *www.osha.gov*.

Chapter Review:

Benefits and Compensation—Be a front line resource to employees. Control labor costs.

Motivation and Job Performance Incentives—When you make the workplace environment a fun place to be, employees will feel good about coming in to work.

Harassment and Other Workplace Issues—Harassment in the workplace is a serious issue. Identify harassment situations to provide a comfortable working environment. Include Human Resources.

Safety and Security—Security: Limit access to the workplace and workstations, Secure all entrance ways to company premises, Keep loading docks properly staffed during business hours, Have a secure place for employee belongings, Identify all guests and unfamiliar visitors, Identify all mail and packages that pass through the department. Safety: Keep office equipment properly maintained, Keep office floors and walkways clear of objects and debris, Limit the height of stacked boxes and items, Keep the office well illuminated, Ensure that all relevant materials and supplies are within reasonable reach.

CHAPTER 9

Practical Application

The practical application is in how you utilize this knowledge in moving forward in your management career. While many of these principles have been proven successful, the knowledge and training to apply these principles in no way can compare to the experience built through years of effort. If something fails, learn from it and move on.

Principles of Leadership

Many motivational speakers will discuss leadership skills and refer to the audience as the leaders of tomorrow. After all, the audience is there to learn how to become motivated leaders. The concept of motivating people to become leaders of tomorrow, however, is severely flawed. I would much rather teach and motivate people to become leaders of today. There is no reason why anyone would have to wait until tomorrow, or some undetermined time in the future, to become a leader. You don't have to wait for the opportunity, or just the right time, to become a leader. You have a choice to be a leader of today. It's not a question of when. It's a question of how.

The main ingredients to leadership are passion and desire. If you have the passion and desire to become a leader, then become one now. Leadership is not the passion and desire for self-glory. Leaders don't stand up and proclaim, "Look at me! I am the leader!" Leaders are grown through action.

Leadership starts with self-discipline. Leadership starts with a passion to go beyond what people think you are capable of doing. It is done not for the self-glory, but for the passion to succeed. And when you do succeed, then people will look and say, "Look at him. He succeeded. How did he do it?" You don't tell people to follow you. You simply show them the way. And if they follow you, then you lead them. If they don't follow you, you give them the guidance to choose. But you can't make their choice for them. Dwight Eisenhower, a Military Five Star General and the Thirty-Fourth President of the United States once said, "You do not lead by hitting people over the head. That's assault, not leadership."

> "You do not lead by hitting people over the head. That's assault, not leadership"
>
> - Dwight D Eisenhower

Leadership is having the understanding of a common goal for the team. Leaders do not do things because it benefits them. Leaders do things to benefit the team. And when people see that, they too will want to do their share to benefit the team. They will follow your lead.

Leaders are not superheroes. Leaders know when and how to ask for help. When asked who will take a project, a leader will step up and grab the opportunity, but will also realize that he needs help and support rather than trying to accomplish it all himself. And when that happens, people will step up and say, "I can help. What do you need from me?" Congratulations. You've just become a leader today.

Leadership is about responsibility and accountability. It is also recognizing that accountability also comes with opportunity. If something goes wrong, leaders take the blame. But leaders also take the opportunity to make it right.

Leadership is about doing things right all the time. No one ever became a leader without first doing things right and building their integrity. People want leaders who have integrity. And to have integrity, you do things right all the time. You don't cheat. You don't cut corners. You don't take the easy way out. You do what is right.

Leadership is about courage. It is the courage to see something that is wrong and try to make it right. A leader does not stray from action because it is "none of his business." Leaders make it their business to learn what is going on and to take action to make sure it is right, even if it is going to anger some people. It takes courage to do that. It takes leadership.

Leadership is inspiration, not aspiration. We all aspire to be great. That's a good thing. But greatness comes from inspiring others. Leaders must inspire greatness in others. That's what leadership is all about. It is to inspire others to be great themselves. And when that happens, those who have become great under your leadership will give you the credit for their success.

This is the true definition of leadership. It does not take much to begin the journey. By understanding the true sense of leadership, you can begin that journey today. Do not be a leader of tomorrow. Be a leader of today.

Conclusion

The desire to perform well and advance in our careers should be a driving force behind our actions. It requires the dedication and discipline towards a goal. The belief in these principles, and the courage to follow through, will build the character and strength necessary to not only to succeed in managing employees, but to succeed in anything you do.

> The desire to perform well and advance in our careers should be a driving force behind our actions.

These principles can apply throughout businesses and organizations of every industry. I invite you to utilize the information contained in this book as a resource for your success. I invite you to learn it and apply these principles in your management career. Most importantly, I invite you to live it in your everyday life.

Go and be the best at what you do.

www.ingramcontent.com/pod-product-compliance
Lightning Source LLC
Chambersburg PA
CBHW030913180526
45163CB00004B/1815